THE L.E.A.R.N.E.D. LEADER -

An Allegory About Navigating Change

Stephanie Olexa, PhD, MBA

Copyright © 2014 by Stephanie Olexa, Lead to the Future

ISBN 978-1-312-56376-6

Table of Contents

Dedication

This book is dedicated to the managers and leaders in business, who are actively pursuing personal excellence in order to be the best they can be. I hope this opens new doors for you. This book would not have been possible without the mindful support of my husband, Seth Weber, who encouraged me through the transitions in my life and my sister, Georgine Olexa, who epitomizes intelligence and trustworthiness. I am blessed to have both of them in my life.

I would like to thank my editor James A. Oliveri for his excellent review and suggestions and my content reviewer, Steven Zebowitz, for his insightful suggestions.

The cover photo was generously provided by Captain Jennifer Kaye of Schooner Woodwind Sailing Cruises, Annapolis, MD, showing the Woodwind schooner during a sunset cruise on the Chesapeake Bay.

If you have suggestions or questions about this book or other books by this author, contact me at solexa1776@aol.com or through my website: www.leadtothefuture.com. I hope to hear from you.

Preface

During my long career, first as a scientist, then as a business executive and entrepreneur, I read hundreds, if not thousands, of books, articles, and magazines, trying to learn that one magical tip, *the one great idea* that would change me from being an amateur to a respected colleague. Surprise. There is no one magic tip. No secret. No single book. It's all of them. It's the conglomerate of learning. But more important, it's not just reading the information but incorporating the ideas into your everyday life and work. It's replacing your old ways of thinking with the new ideas and replacing your old actions with new ones. I learned that reading the books wasn't enough. To incorporate the ideas, I had to actively and consciously put them into my daily routine then reflect on how this new method fit me. I had to modify the methods to fit my style and circumstances. I had to make the ideas *part of me*. This book is a story about fictional characters who travel through a maze of changes, toward leadership and success. The main character is guided through the journey by a professional coach as he becomes a L.E.A.R.N.E.D. Leader.

Introduction: Why Change Leadership Matters

The only thing we know for sure is that everything will change. And, that change will be unpredictable in time and in intensity. What we don't know is how we will react to change. Leaders embrace change with curiosity and optimism, recognizing that only through change can people and situations evolve and become better.

This book is an allegory about a young man who is faced with a challenge and an opportunity. He works with a leadership coach to develop his skills as a L.E.A.R.N.E.D. Leader. By using these skills, he navigates change and leads his team to a better future.

Learned (leŕ-ned) is defined in the Merriam Webster dictionary as "characterized by or associated with learning; erudite, such as a learned scholar."

So, if you are not facing a major change right now, inevitably you will in the future. Practice becoming a L.E.A.R.N.E.D. Leader and be ready to make the most of that change.

Chapter 1: Unexpected Challenges

The Shock

Mike was still sipping his first cup of coffee when his iPhone jangled the Marimba, signaling a call from his office. He glared at the phone. It was his first Saturday off in six months and he was looking forward to taking his wife to a long anticipated exhibit at the Philadelphia Museum of Art.

"Mike, so sorry to bother you but we were just informed that Don Smith passed away of a massive heart attack. Completely unexpected. I know that you were very close. He was much more than just a client to all of us, but we all knew he thought of you as his right hand man."

Mike almost dropped the phone. Cathy Gallagher's voice was quaking as she broke the news. Cathy, the Senior Executive Vice President of MagTech Consulting knew Don Smith as long as Mike did, but Mike was Don's prime contact in the firm. Mike had worked on the Square One Chemical account since he joined MagTech almost ten years ago. When Mike was completely honest with himself, he admitted that it was this account and his relationship with Don Smith that kept him enthusiastic and engaged at work. He had to wake his wife, Marie, and tell her the bad news.

"It's like I lost my father. No… worse. My father died when I was eleven so I never really knew him. Don was only fifty-two years old, just ten years older than me, but he was the mentor for both my professional and my personal life. I know it raised some eyebrows when I asked him to be the best man at our wedding, but to me he *was* the best man in my life."

Mike clung to Marie and whispered, "Sorry, honey, I'm not in the mood to go to the museum. I think I'll head in to the office and see if I can help." Marie hugged him but she knew this pain would last a long time.

Just as Mike was pulling out of the driveway, his cell phone rang again, but this time it was the barking dog ringtone, an unknown caller. "What now?" he thought.

"Michael Townsend? This is Seth Weber. I'm the attorney for Mr. Donald Smith. I'm sorry to be the bearer of bad news. I regret to inform you that Mr. Smith passed away last night from a sudden and massive heart attack."

"Thank you, Mr. Weber. I just heard the news from my supervisor at MagTech Consulting and I'm on my way to our offices now to see how we can help."

"Mr. Townsend, I'm calling to ask if you would agree to meet me at my office at 11:00 this morning. It's critical that we meet as soon as possible."

"What's this about?" Mike asked.

"Mr Townsend, it's best if we discuss this in person."

"Okay, see you then." Mike jotted the address into his iPhone and headed to his office.

The Letter

Mike settled into the plush conference room chair at the law offices of Attorney Seth Weber and Associates. Still reeling from the news of the morning, he barely noticed the diplomas and awards on the walls.

"Mr. Townsend, thank you for agreeing to see me this morning. We're all in shock at the tragic passing of Don Smith. He was loved and respected by everyone who met him. I've had the privilege of being his business and personal attorney for over twenty years. He talked about you many times. To him, you were much more than a trusted consultant and expert. He thought of you as the son he never had." Attorney Weber's eyes were bloodshot and he tried hard to keep his voice as professional as possible.

"The feelings were mutual," said Mike. "He was my mentor and friend. Although I brought technical expertise to his company, he taught me how technical products are brought to market. We learned from each other. I will miss him terribly."

Attorney Weber took his time spreading out four thick manila folders on the polished walnut conference table. From one of the folders he extracted an official-looking large white envelope addressed to Michael Townsend. The flap was initialed with the scrawling monogram of Donald L. Smith and stamped with a notary seal. He silently slid the envelope and a letter opener across the table to Mike. "Please, take your time and read this letter carefully."

Mike picked up the letter and held it for a quiet moment, remembering his mentor and closest friend. His eyes blurred with tears.

January 3, 2012
Dear Mike:

If you are reading this, I'm dead. Sorry to be so blunt, but I was hoping that someday I would have the chance to invite you to my retirement and seventieth birthday party, then tear up this letter. Oh, well. I asked Attorney Weber to arrange to meet with you privately and give you this letter within twenty-four hours of my passing. It will become obvious why time is of the essence.

Mike, when I first met you, I realized that you had a special gift. Your creativity and leadership skills were amazing for one so young. I watched you further develop those skills while growing in technical and business acumen. You are also the most trustworthy individual I have ever met. What a combination! Stop blushing or denying. You can't argue with a dead guy! But this is why I'm asking you to finish my legacy.

As you know, I started Square One Chemical right after finishing my MBA. The business was my mistress and fortunately, my wonderful wife Anne, was never jealous. Anne was there for me in the bad times and cheered for me in the good times. I see that Marie gives you that same kind of loving support. We are blessed to have these wonderful women in our lives!

I grew the business without taking on investors or partners. I built a company that I loved. I enjoyed every fourteen-hour day and would be working today if I hadn't croaked. (Sorry for the bad humor.) Honestly, I loved being the person in charge, the big cheese, the go-to person, and I did not want to share that. If I

4

had, I could have torn up this letter (or not needed to write it in the first place). Oh, well.... again!

So the problem with being the "one and only" is that if the worst case scenario happens and the big cheese doesn't get to retire gracefully, then the business that I loved so much is at risk of suddenly closing. I care for my dedicated staff and loyal customers far too much to let that happen, so Attorney Weber helped me to craft this plan. I hope you will agree to be part of the solution.

Square One has been growing dramatically over the past several years and my key managers are talented and dedicated to the company. They are great, don't get me wrong. But none of them has the ability...that certain something... needed to step up and lead the company in my absence. They will need a new leader. I think you are that leader.

Upon my death, the one thousand shares of stock that are in my name will pass to my wife, Anne. I also purchased a ten million dollar life insurance policy and made Square One the beneficiary. With that bucket of money, the company will purchase from my wife four hundred and ninety-nine shares for eight million dollars. So forty-nine percent of the stock will become treasury stock for a future earn-out by the new CEO and Anne will retain the controlling interest. The remaining two million dollars will be available to fund the company through the transition, pay the new CEO and finish my dream of growing the company.

I am asking you to become the new CEO, and eventually, co-owner of Square One. This is not the kind of decision that I expect you to make on the spot. But, I do need someone to take charge of the company immediately. So, I am proposing that Square One hire you as interim CEO on assignment from

MagTech Consulting for a period of six months. Attorney Weber has also prepared a letter to MagTech offering a substantial payment for your services for six months. If, at the end of the six months, you decide that this is not for you, then you can collaborate with MagTech to form a search committee to find the new CEO. You would be free to go back to MagTech, or do whatever next step works for you. Anne and I would be grateful for your interim service. But, if you choose to stay, you will get a substantial salary and options for all of the treasury shares to be earned out over a ten year period. At that time you will be able to buy out Anne's shares and become "the new big cheese". The company's current Board of

Directors (except, of course, Anne will take my place) will continue to support and assist you to set strategy, goals and milestones. The Board will approve the award of your options annually, based on your performance against the agreed upon goals. All options will vest at the end of ten years.

For you this is an opportunity and a challenge. Or as Mr. Monk would say, "a curse and a blessing". For me, it is a way to ensure the continuation of the business I love, through the hands of someone I trust.

Stepping up to lead an organization of this size is a challenge, so your old mentor offers you this "sage" advice:

Don't be too proud to ask for help.

Follow your passion.

Take care of yourself, mentally and physically.

Treasure Marie. You will need her by your side, regardless of the decisions you make.

You are surrounded by people who want you to succeed. Trust them.

Thank you, Mike. I trust you with my legacy.

Your friend,
Don

The Funeral

Gentle wisps of white smoke announced the smell of the incense as the priest circled the dark walnut casket. Mike dabbed his eyes with his shredded tissues. Marie's hand rested on his knee and she gave it a gentle squeeze. Mike was still in shock and Marie was the anchor that would get him through this. Saying goodbye to his mentor was tough and he was also feeling the weight of Don's request on his shoulders. He and Marie were up until almost dawn talking about every aspect of what could be in store for them. At sun up, Mike and Marie hugged and promised each other that they would honor Don's legacy as best they could. Mike felt compelled to write a letter back to Don to formalize his commitment. As he listened to the final prayer, he caressed the sealed envelope. Later, he would put the letter in the secret compartment of his antique roll top desk.

The Day After the Funeral
Tuesday 8:00 am

Anne Smith looked exhausted and pale. Her simple black suit seemed to hang on her thin frame. "Good Morning, everyone. First, I want to thank you for your kind words, the flowers and the contributions to *Animals In Distress* to honor Don. You know he loved each of you. You were, no *are*, our family. Although Don's death was unexpected and untimely, he was always prepared. As part of his estate, he had specific instructions as to what to do in the case of his unplanned passing, so that all of you, his suppliers and his customers could continue on with just a minor hiccup. He cared. *Really* cared. So, I'm here this morning to tell you not to worry about your jobs or the impact of this event on your families. Square One will continue. I realize you all know Mike Townsend from MagTech Consulting. Mike has been not only a technical resource for Don but also a trusted advisor. As of today Mike will be the interim CEO of Square One. I will be taking Don's place on the Board and Mike will report directly to the Board. This is what Don wanted. I know that you will give Mike your full support and build on the company's foundation to reach even greater success in the future. Please join me in welcoming Mike."

The applause barely drowned out the sigh of relief from the staff. They all knew that Don was the sole owner of the company and most of them had been overwhelmed with both grief and fear since they heard the news. The realization that Don thought about them and had planned for their futures caused many of the staff to again reach for their tissues.

"Good morning, everyone. All of us are feeling great pain at the loss of our friend, colleague, and mentor." Mike's voice quivered and broke. He didn't even try to hide his tears. It was a few minutes before he could speak again.

"But, this company was Don's joy, his passion and as he said, the second love of his life." Mike reached for Anne's hand and gave it a gentle squeeze. "For his sake and for his wonderful wife, Anne's, sake we will continue to grow this company. It is an honor to be the interim CEO for the next six months. My first priority is to get to know all of you, what you do and how you do it. Then, we will work on a plan for moving forward. I can't tell you that this will be easy or smooth. I will make mistakes. But please know that I have the best intentions and the commitment to give all of us a great future. Now, let's get to work and make Don proud."

As the crowd dispersed, they hugged Anne and shook Mike's hand, many of them jokingly calling him "Boss". Anne and Mike exchanged weak smiles, then headed to Don's office to make the painful transition.

Chapter 2: The Adventure Begins

Day One Ends

Finally quiet. Mike sat in what was Don's office and sighed heavily. "The adventure begins," he said, not just to himself but to the photo hanging on the wall of Don accepting the Entrepreneur of the Year Award. He spent his first day introducing himself to all the employees then making calls to the Board members. The names and faces were a blur right now, but he knew that over the next few weeks things would fall into place.

Although he had been working as a consultant to Don for ten years, Mike realized that he knew only a small portion of the overall business. He needed to wrap his hands around the full scope of the company, understand where the organization was headed and work with the Board to be sure that it was the right direction.

"Step one, get to know the management team," Mike said with a semi-confident smile toward the photo.

Mike pulled out the personnel files from the cabinet under the window. Although his stomach was grumbling and he could almost smell Marie's tortellini Alfredo, he planned to settle in for an hour or so just to get a quick background on the key people. He saw the staff starting to trickle out at 5:15 and assumed it would soon be quiet. He laid out the files of the management team:

Eric Miller, Director of Finance

Sally Jones, Director of Human Resources

Jessica White, Director of Marketing

John Black, Director of Sales

Todd Wall, Director of Operations

Alan Atkins, Director of Research and Development

Jennifer Brown, Director of Quality

Just as Mike finished arranging the folders on his desk, Eric, the Director of Finance, tapped on the door and stepped in. His arms were loaded with papers and binders.

"Hi, Mike. Sorry to bother you at the end of your first day in the hot seat, but I need a few signatures. First, here is the signature card for the bank so you can sign company checks. I'll run it over to the bank on my way home tonight. Then, this stack of checks needs to be signed so I can have my secretary mail them tomorrow morning. I've attached the documentation to each check so you know the basis for each expense. Here are the authorization forms for your approval for the purchase order requests from production and R&D so we can call out supply orders tomorrow. Todd and Alan are jumping all over me to get some of these items in. And, finally, here is the summary of the quotes for the health care coverage for next year. You need to decide whether to continue with our current coverage or change carriers before next Wednesday so I can get all the forms to Sally for the employees to fill out. Sorry to hit you with so much all at once, but I've got to tell you, it's like this most days."

Mike's desk was now covered with the purchase orders, expense reports, checks and binders from insurance providers.

He glanced at the clock. No way would he make it home before midnight.

"I'd better call Marie," Mike sighed to himself. "Life is going to be a lot different for both of us." The imagined smell of Marie's Tortellini Alfredo was beginning to fade.

Day Two - Wednesday

Fine. It was slightly after midnight when Mike left the office, but he was not about to saunter in after the staff arrived the next morning. At 7:00 am, only the workers on the early shift in the manufacturing area were in the building.

"I will work harder, longer and smarter than anyone and I won't let them see me sweat." Mike said it out loud, but nobody heard it.

At 8:01am, Eric poked his head in the door. "Got those checks, boss?" With a big smile, Eric picked up the results of Mike's late night and headed back to his office.

"Oops."

"Hey, I was here first." Mike looked up to see John and Jennifer jockeying for position at his door.

"OK, Ladies first. I'll come back in about ten minutes," John said as he headed back to his office.

"Good morning, Jen. What can I do for you?"

Mike quickly went over his mental file on Jen. Jennifer Brown, Director of Quality, BA from Georgetown and MBA from University of Pennsylvania with a specialty in Quality Systems. Don had hired her about three years ago and it looked like she had made some significant improvements in product quality in a short time.

"Join me in some coffee?" Mike asked.

With a quick shake of her head, Jen dismissed the offer of coffee and handed Mike a thick file. "Well, here's the situation. Don had asked me to put together a summary of what it would take to have our manufacturing facility ISO 9001 compliant. I

14

prepared this table of the key elements and what we would have to do. I have to tell you, it's a bit overwhelming. Our manufacturing documentation would need a complete overhaul. We make great products but the additional paperwork would add a lot of time and effort to production. I don't know if you can convince Todd to go along with it. But, here's the report." With a somewhat shy smile, Jen turned and headed to the door. "Let me know what you want to do."

Impressive, Mike thought as he thumbed through Jen's report. Well outlined, clear comparisons of current versus proposed structure, but it seemed to stop short of a recommendation or an action plan.

"My turn," John said with a grin. "Just wanted to give you this sales report. The key issue is that the Stellar Products contract is up for renewal. It was a three year contract with a three year automatic extension that included a no-price-increase guarantee. Our margins are good but could be better. When I propose the new contract, do you want me to keep the pricing the same, have a small increase or decrease the prices to ensure that they don't look around for a new supplier? I hear that Quality Chemical Company has been aggressively pricing their products this year. Stellar has been a loyal customer for over ten years, but times they are a changin'. We have a meeting scheduled next Friday at their offices so you have a few days to think about it. But, if you could let me know as soon as you decide, I'd appreciate it. I like to get the paperwork ready for signature and bring it to the meeting."

John was half-way out the door when he turned and said, "Thanks, Boss."

"I may have a few questions. I'm not familiar with this account. I was planning to meet with each of the managers anyway so I can get my questions together and we can talk about it then. How about 2:00 today?"

"Sure thing, Boss."

The door didn't have a chance to click closed behind John, when it was tugged open by Alan, Director of R & D.

"Hey. I know you and Don had been working on the scale-up of the Lupine Oil process so I need to know if you want me to proceed with ordering the capital equipment for the project. Here are the quotes and the total installed costs are going to be about $265,000. The lead times are eight to ten weeks, so the sooner we get the orders placed, the better."

"Alan, can we talk about this tomorrow morning at 9:00. There are some other things I want to review with you so can you set aside about two hours?"

"No problem."

Two scheduled, five to go, thought Mike. His desk was again piled high. Mike's head was spinning and it was only 9:30.

Let the Meetings Begin

Mike plowed his way through the first pile by 11:30 and rewarded himself by taking a long, slow walk through the manufacturing floor to see the action and relieve the kink in his neck. Todd Wall, Director of Operations was in his office, frowning at the computer screen, with a line of old Starbucks cups at the edge of his desk. Todd's office resembled a company museum, with framed patents, product ads, awards and customers letters on all the walls. Mike looked at the row of binders on the shelf behind Todd with dates going back over twenty years. Don had hired Todd when the business moved to this location and the company was in a significant growth period. Don and Todd were close friends as well as colleagues. They "learned" the business together, through trial and error. They graduated as "fraternity brothers from the college of seat of the pants" as Don liked to tell it. Mike took one look at Todd's face and realized how deeply affected he was by Don's passing.

Todd's expertise in chemical operations was well established. The company's safety and environmental record was flawless. Todd ran a tight ship and was respected by the fifty or so staff in his department. During Mike's years of consulting with Square One he had worked with Todd closely and admired his dedication and skill.

"Hello, Todd. Mind if I interrupt for a minute?" Without waiting for an answer, Mike stepped in and dropped into the side chair. "I want to schedule a bit of time with you so I can get up to speed. Are you available tomorrow at 1:00?"

"Sure. Anything in particular you want to review?"

"Let's start with a year-to-date manufacturing update and your projections for the next two quarters."

"You got it," Todd answered without looking up.

" Thanks."

On his way back to his office, Mike poked his head into Jennifer's door. "Hi, Jen. Got a minute? I have a few questions about the report you gave me."

Jen spun around in her chair and gave him a big grin. "So, what's the next step, Boss?"

"I was just about to ask you the same question. I was really impressed with your analysis of the challenge and what it would take to get the ISO 9001 accreditation. This would give us a huge advantage in some of the emerging applications of our processes, but it does have ripple effects across the organization. What feedback did you get from Todd, Eric and Jessica?"

Jen's gaze dropped to the papers on her desk. "Well, they haven't seen the report yet. Don wanted me to give him the briefing first."

"Got it. OK, let's go over some of the details so I really understand it."

Mike spent almost two hours with Jen and was even more impressed with her analytical skills and knowledge of the regulatory processes. Her record-keeping skills were awesome and she seemed to have a good rapport with outside auditors. She presented a very balanced picture of the pros and cons of going forward with the ISO 9001 certification.

"Thanks Jen. I appreciate the time today. Let me spend some more time with your report and get back to you. You're a huge asset to this organization. Oops. Gotta run. I'm meeting John in a few minutes."

Mike took a quick "bio break", grabbed a cup of coffee and headed toward John's office.

John was leaning back in his chair with spreadsheets covering not only his desk, but most of the floor space as well. Mike carefully stepped around what looked to be an abstract art display of data. John was another one of the long term employees with over ten years with the company. He led a team of eight sales staff who covered the US and international markets. In addition, he had over thirty key distributors in Europe and Asia. Don always said that John could sell bikinis to Eskimos in winter by capturing their imaginations and convincing them that they would be prepared for global warming. Don believed that the rapid growth of the specialty products division of the company over the past six years was because John had aggressively attacked the emerging markets in Asia.

"So, John, tell me about the Stellar Products proposal. What are you thinking?" Mike said as he moved a stack of sales reports from the side chair.

"Well, they are our single largest customer, representing over five million dollars in sales this year and growing. They had a three year contract with one three-year automatic extension. That extension is now coming to an end and they asked me to propose a new contract. Since the first contract was signed six years ago we have raised our prices on those products to other customers but held steady for Stellar because of the "no escalation" clause in the agreement. So, do you want me to hold to the old price or increase prices to our current prices or even, yikes, decrease the prices to be sure to keep the volume?"

Mike thought for a minute then asked, "How important are our materials in their final product?" Then Mike slowly added,

"And, what substitutes do they have? What are their projections for growth of their sales in the future?"

John flushed then in a hesitating voice said, "I don't know, because Don had all that information. I'm just the sales director. I know that I've run into Quality Chemical Company reps out on the road. In fact, I remember recognizing one of their reps listed on the sign-in book at Stellar when I stopped by last month. But I'm not sure who else might be sniffing around Stellar. The rest of the info? Check with Jessica in marketing, maybe she knows."

Mike could feel his blood pressure rising sharply. The largest customer? John didn't know how the customer was using their products? He wasn't getting future projections from the customer? He didn't know who the competitors were? What was going on?

"When is the proposal due? I'll try to get more information and we can talk about it later."

"The proposal is due in a week. I think you're getting the picture of how things are done around here," John said as he went back to his spreadsheets.

Mike was about to leave but turned back to John and asked, "What are all these spreadsheets?"

"Rerouting and returns of products," John answered with a frustrated sigh.

Although John's parting comment caused Mike's heart to skip a beat...or three...he had to focus on the Stellar Products proposal. Five million dollars a year was almost five percent of total revenue. If the contract was not renewed and Square One took a five million dollar hit on the sales level it would be devastating to profitability. It certainly would squash his plans for growth and stability for the next six months. "I'd better talk to

Jessica White, pronto," Mike said to himself as he headed back toward his office.

As Mike approached his office he saw Eric standing there with a stack of paperwork. Eric smiled and said, "Yup, Boss, today's checks for review and signing and purchase order requests. Not as many as yesterday and only a few need to be rushed."

Mike looked at his schedule for Thursday. Alan at 9:00 and Todd at 1:00. Could he fit a meeting with Jessica at 3:30? "It'll have to happen. The Stellar Proposal can't wait," Mike mumbled.

Mike's first call was to Jessica to schedule the meeting for the next afternoon. His second call was to his wife, Marie, and for just a few minutes he felt normal again.

Marie Waits Up

Eleven forty-five PM. Mike was always home by 6:00 pm. Marie looked at the clock every ten minutes. He said he would be home late again but she hadn't heard from him since 5:30 pm. They always had dinner together. It was a promise they made to each other when they got married. They would keep their relationship special even when their careers got crazy. They described dinner together as the calm between storms. Two nights in a row and no Mike. No dinner. Not home till midnight. Is this a temporary blip or will life be different now? Marie's eyes blurred. She wasn't sure if it was tears or just fatigue.

Is It Really Only Day Three?

Mike looked at the calendar again. Thursday. Only Thursday? Mike's bloodshot eyes were evidence of his lack of sleep. When he got home at almost 1:30 in the morning, Marie was asleep and he was too exhausted to eat the dinner she had set out for him. Dinner with Marie. Marie loved to cook and he loved to eat. They always told friends that it was a match made in heaven...or at least at the grocery store. He missed sharing the quiet time over food, talking not only about the events of the day, but about their dreams and plans. Who would have guessed that chicken cordon bleu was a big part of the secret of a happy marriage? "Will we ever be able to get back to that?" Mike whispered to himself, "Is this worth it?"

His late night work did clear his desk. He had dropped off the pile of checks and purchase orders on Eric's desk on his way out of the building and had a clean space of almost three feet by three feet in the center of his desk. Maybe things were looking up.

The Lupine Oil project file was at least three inches thick. He had spent about two hours with it the previous night and had prepared a list of questions for Alan for their 9:00 am meeting. Before this project, Mike thought Lupines were only a pretty, spiky perennial flower in gardens. He learned that the Lupine bean is a commercial crop with increasing popularity. The highest-value products are edible refined Lupine oil and high quality Lupine flour. Lupine flour was developed into a high protein meat supplement that could be made into food products with a texture that is moist and chewy. The edible oil could be used as most vegetable oils in cooking but the highly refined version has been identified as a potential natural cosmetic with the ability to protect the skin against sun damage. It's being touted as a miracle, all-natural anti-aging compound. Alan's proposal focused on producing the highly refined oil with the flour as a valuable by-product of the process. From Mike's perspective, it looked like a very novel and cost effective process. Mike knew that the company was looking for a way to enter new, high value-added markets, like the emerging nutraceuticals market, and this product would be a good entry point. Now he understood why Don had asked Jen to develop the ISO 9001 plan. To be successful as a supplier of active ingredients in the pharmaceutical or cosmetic industry the company would have to have ISO 9001 certification and have FDA approval. The challenge was not just developing the extraction and purification process for the products, but changing the organization to be competitive in a highly regulated industry and to sell on the basis of product performance, not just low price. This project was a door into a new industry, but making the most of the opportunity would be a huge challenge throughout the organization.

Mike took the heavy file with him to Alan's office. "Wow, Alan, I understand why you're so pumped about this project," Mike said. "I have a few questions, but from the way you outlined the process, it seems to be both doable and efficient. Can we talk about how this would impact the rest of production and the Quality Assurance group?"

A broad smile crept across Alan's face. "I'm glad you picked up on my vision, Boss," said Alan as he pulled out even more data on the process. His enthusiasm was sincere. Alan really believed in this project and was willing to commit to making it happen. After all his questions had been answered...in great detail...Mike stood to leave.

"What kind of feedback have you gotten from the rest of the management team?" Mike asked.

"You're the only one who has seen this proposal. Don knew it would be somewhat... no hugely, disruptive to the status quo if we went ahead with this, so he wanted to make a decision before he dropped the bomb on the rest of the staff. I think you should be prepared for some push-back from the production team and especially from the sales group. A change of this magnitude will be like trying to convince Amtrak that a kids train in the Central Park Zoo would be a good addition to their network."

Mike sighed with relief knowing that Alan was in tune with both the size of this opportunity but also with the difficulty of making changes throughout the organization in order to make it happen. "My thoughts exactly," said Mike, "except I was envisioning a merger between Cirque de Soleil and Ringling Brothers."

"Yeah, you get it, Boss," Alan said with a small laugh, "you have a tough decision to make."

"No, Alan, WE have a tough decision to make. All of us. If the entire team doesn't commit to this vision, then we're wasting our time." Mike's words fell like hailstones on the metal roof of an airplane hangar, leaving an ominous echo that seemed to hang in the air.

Mike glanced at his watch and saw that he had about forty minutes before his meeting with Todd. He dropped the Lupine Oil file on his desk, checked voice mail and wrote quick responses to all eight of the emails that had the word "urgent" in the subject line. One of the emails was from their supplier of a high purity acid that was an ingredient in a specialty formulation that they made for the electronics industry. The supplier was notifying all customers that over the previous weekend they had a major fire at their manufacturing plant in China. Mike had to spend some time looking at the impact this would have on their production.

Mike's work with Don over the years focused mainly on supply chain management. As a manufacturer of specialty chemicals, Square One had to source key raw materials from around the world. Mike helped Don to find these suppliers and negotiate pricing and delivery terms. Mike had also done the annual on-site inspections of each of the suppliers to ensure quality. Don had accompanied him on some of those trips so Mike had a chance to get to know him well. Nothing creates friendships like trying to find a decent burger a hundred miles from the nearest city in mainland China. They also spent time together, accompanied by their wives, at the theater and at restaurants. During all of those times, Don seemed absorbed, focused but never relaxed. Now, Mike understood the weight that Don was carrying. In the old days, Mike would be able to focus all of his attention on the problem caused by the fire at their supplier's factory. Now, it was just one item on an ever-growing list.

As he headed out of the door for his meeting with Todd, he glanced at the photo of Don on the wall and said to himself "How did you do this for so long, my friend?"

Mike felt comfortable in Todd's office. Maybe it was the familiarity with Square One from his consulting time or maybe it was because of Mike's own background in engineering and operations. Mike had spent time with Todd working on the raw material specification sheets, the quality requirements and the delivery terms. But now, Mike was sitting in Todd's office in a different role, wearing the President's hat, not a consultant's hat.

Suddenly it struck him that he only knew a piece of production, the piece that intersected with supply chain management.

"Todd, thanks for setting aside time to bring me up to date. As I walked in here today, I realized that I don't have a complete picture of production here. I know your supply chain like the back of my hand, but that's about it," said Mike as he settled into the side chair.

"I'm in the same boat," said Todd, "I don't know the details of the supply chain that you managed. I saw the email that you forwarded this morning about the fire and the possible effect on the availability of high purity acid. Just what we need right now, another emergency."

Mike shook his head in agreement and walked to the whiteboard. He drew a series of interlocking gears surrounding one large gear on the whiteboard. "I'm getting the feeling that this is the operational plan for the company. Each person spinning in their own circle and interacting with one or a small number of people in a peripheral way but pretty oblivious to how things fit together," Mike said.

"That's it. Don was the central repository of information and decision making," Todd said. "Don't get me wrong. It worked well, really well. For as long as Don was here, anyway. You know I've been here for over twenty years and I guess the system just evolved. Don was the entrepreneur, the one with the vision. We didn't question him. He was brilliant and the hardest working person I've ever met. But he kept all the responsibility on his own shoulders. He would often tell me that he made the decision to start the business and the rest of us should not suffer for his decision. He said he wanted to 'protect' us from the worry and stress. He wouldn't accept that we wanted to help. And, that maybe if we were more involved, it would reduce the stress for everyone. It would not have been laying a burden on us. It would have been an honor to share the load. But, why am I telling you this? You wanted to see the year-to-date production update and the projections for the next two quarters. Let's start there."

After about an hour and a half, Mike stood up and stretched. "As I expected, Todd, this is a well-run operation. You have efficient scheduling and no apparent bottlenecks. Your time from order to shipment is excellent."

"Thanks. I have a great team and Jen Brown has brought some excellent new procedures for in-process quality control. Her six sigma and lean training have been a great supplement to the department."

"I was with John yesterday reviewing the sales projections. He had a lot of data spread out and threw out a comment that it was data on rerouting and returns. I haven't had a chance to get details yet. Do you know what that is all about?"

"I think so. Our biggest customer for high purity etchants is ST Electronics Company. They had a standing order for three of our products so our contract said to ship a set amount to each of their facilities on a pre-determined schedule. Well, they've been hit by some tough competition so they're making changes. First, they consolidated two production facilities into one. Of course, we didn't know that, so we continued to ship to the original location. They can't transport the material from the original location to the new one because they don't have a license from the Department of Transportation to move hazardous materials, so we had to make arrangements to have the materials reshipped to the new location. Then, they began some process changes and the product we shipped didn't work anymore. We needed to bring it back in-house and repurify it to a higher standard. It's been a huge problem for about five months. The worst of it is that my

28

gut tells me they are trying to eliminate one of our products from their process. That one product makes up the majority of the volume and, according to Don, is the highest margin product. None of our other customers for the product have given us an indication that they are also looking to eliminate it from their processes. But, that industry is not very good at keeping secrets so if ST Electronics finds a way, the rest of the industry won't be far behind."

"John didn't mention anything about this. I'll have to dig deeper with him," said Mike, "but it sounds like a big issue for us."

"You'll have to check with Eric but I think that overall, that one product is about eight percent of our revenue," said Todd with a somber look on his face.

Mike got up slowly and glanced at his watch. Almost 3:30. "I'm meeting with Jessica in just a few minutes. I'll find out what kind of intel she has on the industry."

On his way to Jessica's office, Mike stopped in the lunch room to grab some coffee. As he savored the deep aroma of his favorite brew he jotted some notes in his book.

BIG ISSUES

1. Electronics product displaced by customer (ST Electronics) = 8% decrease in revenue ???
2. Stellar Products contract renewal = 5% risk to revenue.
3. Lupine Oil production = ?? increase in revenue.
4. Lupine Oil capital cost = $265,000 !!!!!
5. Cost of ISO 9001 and FDA approval = ??
6. Rerouting and rework of product = cost??

"Jessica, can I get you some coffee?" Mike asked as he put his cup on the edge of Jessica's desk.

"Thanks, but no, I'm caffeined out. What can I do for you?"

"I'd like to spend a bit of time to get to know you. I saw in your file that your MBA in marketing is from Ohio State. Great school. And, you spent almost ten years in the chemical industry before coming to Square One three years ago. How's my memory?"

"Perfect. My previous employer was a huge chemical company, so I did get to see a variety of approaches to marketing in this industry. But, I spent most of my time as the head of marketing for the methanol product line. It was a tough business. We had a good product and rapid response to the customer but pennies counted. Actually, only the pennies mattered. The customers made their buying decisions only on the basis of price. There were four producers so we found ourselves in cut-throat bidding most of the time. It was nice to come here and experience a smaller organization and some specialty products."

"That was the perfect opening for my questions, thanks," Mike said. "Tell me about the product mix, what's the competitive advantage for the major products and where is the market going?"

Jessica spun around in her chair and pulled a chart from the file cabinet. "This is what Don and I have been discussing for a while."

By Volume By Revenue

| | Base Products | Specialty Formulations | Proprietary Products |

"Our base products are commodities. That means that a lot of suppliers make them and we compete on price. Our customers bid out their requirements each year and we keep sharpening our pencils to get a lower and lower price. On some of these products we barely make a profit. It's very frustrating because you can see from this chart that they make up over fifty percent of our volume but only twenty four percent of our revenue. The specialty formulations are products that we mix using know-how we developed over the years. They make up forty-two percent of our volume but over fifty percent of our revenue. And our proprietary products are the ones that we make with our own special techniques, making us key suppliers, or in some cases, sole suppliers, to our customers. They are just eight percent of our volume but twenty-five percent of our revenue."

"I'm not surprised at the trend," said Mike, "Don's goal was to move the company into more specialty and proprietary products because they have much better profit margins and less competition. But, I am surprised that we are still producing so many low-profit products."

"Don and I had been talking about this for a while. He was struggling with the decision. Eric can fill you in on the financial details."

"Thanks, Jessica," Mike said. "You helped me to get the big picture of where we are ...and maybe where we need to go."

Mike added another item to his growing list.

BIG ISSUES
1. Electronics product displaced by customer (ST Electronics) = 8% decrease in revenue ???
2. Stellar Products contract renewal = 5% risk to revenue.
3. Lupine Oil production = ?? increase in revenue.
4. Lupine Oil capital cost = $265,000 !!!!!
5. Cost of ISO 9001 and FDA approval = ??
6. Rerouting and rework of product = cost??
7. Should we be making all these base products or stop??

Day Four - TGIF

Friday. 6:55 am. Mike booted up his computer. Mike's determination to show the staff that he was dedicated to the company was taking a toll. Another missed dinner with Marie, late night and now an early start. But, he'd have two hours to review the paperwork on the health care renewal proposals before he met with Sally at 9:00.

Mike had met Sally on his first visit to MagTech. She had started as Don's receptionist almost twenty years ago. The company was small and everyone wore at least ten hats. Sally became Don's secretary and took over some of the bookkeeping. Then, about six years ago she became head of Human Resources. She had a motherly approach that gave the staff the confidence that she was always looking out for them. Mike realized that Sally must be in her sixties now. "Yikes," Mike said to himself, "I wonder if Don's passing will make Sally think of retiring."

The two hours flew by and Mike found himself settling into a side chair in Sally's office.

"I reviewed these proposals, Sally. I'm surprised at the price increases for next year. Do you know why the big change?"

"We've had a few employees with serious illnesses in the past year. There was Toby in sales with the difficult childbirth and her baby was in the NICU for almost three months. And, Bill in production was diagnosed with kidney cancer. Fortunately both are doing well now, but their expenses were high. That could have had an effect. Or maybe, Obamacare....who knows? But, you're right. This is the highest change we have seen in about five years."

"Let's go with the Big Blue plan for the year. We can look at it again next year and maybe get some reduction if our experience numbers get better."

Sally took the Big Blue proposal and ceremoniously tossed the rest into the trash bin. "Mike, just before Don passed, he and I had some difficult conversations about the production staff for the base products. He said that profitability in those products has been decreasing and asked me to get together some figures on the cost of a layoff. This was very confidential. I don't think he had made a decision, just wanted to know the magnitude of the cost if it went that way."

"Thanks, Sally. I understand why he asked you to look at this. I don't know how he was leaning or what he planned, but I'm going to be spending a lot of time on this issue in the next few weeks. I really appreciate that you have this data ready. And, I *really* appreciate keeping this quiet until we have some time to make a good decision."

Sally's smile showed her appreciation for the complement.

"I do have another question, Sally." Mike paused. He wasn't sure how to broach the subject. Finally he said. "I know you and Don were very close so I'm sure his passing so suddenly hit you like a ton of bricks and I'm worried about you."

Sally's eyes quickly brimmed with tears. "Oh, Mr. Townsend," she said with a catch in her voice. "It knocked me for a loop. I'm not sure how I'll get my bearings again. I'm not saying anything against you, of course, but I'm doing some soul searching. Honestly, retirement did cross my mind. I'll be 65 in four months. Maybe I should spend more time with my grandkids. Who knows if I'll be next?"

"Oh, Sally, you have been part of the foundation of this company since the beginning. It would be a huge loss to all of us if you left. But I understand. I'm going to ask a personal favor and ask that you commit to stay through the transition, six months. I'll respect your decision on your plans after that."

"I owe that to Don. You can count on me for at least the next six months...God willing and the cricks don't rise."

Mike hugged Sally and took the file. It was a thin blue folder with a few pages inside, but it felt surprisingly heavy. He pulled out his notebook and added two more lines to his worry list.

BIG ISSUES
1. Electronics product displaced by customer (ST Electronics) = 8% decrease in revenue ???
2. Stellar Products contract renewal = 5% risk to revenue.
3. Lupine Oil production = ?? increase in revenue.
4. Lupine Oil capital cost = $265,000 !!!!!
5. Cost of ISO 9001 and FDA approval = ??
6. Rerouting and rework of product = cost??
7. Should we be making all these base products or stop??
8. Was Don planning a layoff?
9. What to do if Sally decides to retire?

Mike headed back to his office and started thinking about the meatloaf sandwich he had made that morning. When he got home the previous night, the smell of his missed dinner with Marie enveloped the kitchen. Eating the leftover today was not the same....not even close.

By 1:00 Mike was in Eric's office. As the Chief Financial Officer, Eric had a better picture of the overall operation than anyone else in the company. Eric was with the company for over five years and Don relied on his ability to manage cash flow during the growth they had experienced recently. Eric had great relationships with the bank as well as with the Board. He had an MBA from the Wharton School at University of Pennsylvania and had about ten years of experience in the chemical industry. Mike wondered why Don had not chosen Eric as the acting President. He also wondered why Eric was not pissed that Don didn't select him.

"Hey, Boss, you've been putting in long hours," Eric said with a smile. "I know you want to go over the financials for the past year and the budget for the next three quarters so I put together these tables. I'd like to give you an overview then we can dig deeper into particular areas."

Mike was impressed with the detailed reports that Eric laid out. The graphs made the trends obvious.

"I guess you spoke to Todd and Jessica about the issues in the base product lines. Let me show you the financial impact on the company," Eric said as he spread out several pages of data.

Eric's graph with converging lines of revenue and costs for the base product lines were steeper and more dramatic than Mike had expected from his conversations with the rest of the team.

"It's worse than I thought," Mike said. "With these trajectories, the entire product line will be taking a huge loss by the end of the year. And from your data, it seems that the growth in the specialty and proprietary products won't save the day."

"Unfortunately, I think that's the bottom line…no pun intended," said Eric.

"Tell me about your discussions about this with Don. What were his plans?"

"That's also part of the problem. This is not a surprise. I made sure that Don was aware of the downward trend as soon as it was definitive. For a long time, he put his head in the sand, refused to admit it. He kept telling me that he would wait just one more quarter before making any big decisions. But three weeks ago when he saw the most recent changes he had to admit that we had to look hard at the base business products. Honestly, I wasn't shocked that Don had a heart attack. He was working non-stop and he seemed to be on a treadmill. Maybe he thought that if he worked longer and harder he could change the world. This is the first time the company hit a real roadblock and he was having a hard time coming to terms with it. A layoff? Unthinkable. 'Not on my watch' he would say. It was tearing him apart. But we couldn't do anything to change the dynamics of the electronics industry. And, I guess Don knew this day would eventually come but I think that he convinced himself that it wouldn't be this big of an impact."

"Thanks for being so open, Eric. I appreciate your unbiased opinions on this issue. We have some tough decisions to make."

"We?" Eric asked with a tone of sarcasm. "Maybe I shouldn't be so blunt. But, you said you wanted the real scoop. That was another one of the problems here. Don did everything. Don made all of the decisions. I don't want to sound pompous, but I'm a smart guy. I could have, no should have, had more input into the direction of the company. In fact, Todd, Jessica and Alan all felt the same way. "You do *your* job and I'll do *mine*" is what Don always said. I felt like a spoke on a wheel. Don was the hub and the rest of us were spokes. We never knew what the other spokes were doing. I felt like I was in a box in the back of a UPS truck, nice inside my box but had no idea where the truck was headed and what other boxes were in the truck. I think I just gave you two different analogies or mixed metaphors or whatever. But I think you know what I'm getting at. I had this conversation with Don. He knew how I was feeling and I think he knew, or suspected, that I was looking for a job outside the company."

Eric's face was flushed and he fidgeted with the pens on his desk.

"Eric, when I said 'we', I meant 'we'. I agree. You are a smart guy and you really know this business. You have my promise. I will not be making any big decisions behind closed doors. I need the team to run this company."

"OK, thanks, Boss," said Eric as Mike walked out.

Mike was shaken by Eric's outburst. He grabbed another cup of coffee on his way back to his office. After slumping into his chair he pulled out the list of big issues. Two more.

BIG ISSUES

1. Electronics product displaced by customer (ST Electronics) = 8% decrease in revenue ???
2. Stellar Products contract renewal = 5% risk to revenue.
3. Lupine Oil production = ?? increase in revenue.
4. Lupine Oil capital cost = $265,000 !!!!!
5. Cost of ISO 9001 and FDA approval = ??
6. Rerouting and rework of product = cost??
7. Should we be making all these base products or stop??
8. Was Don planning a layoff?
9. What to do if Sally decides to retire?
10. Is the company headed for big financial trouble?
11. Is Eric really planning to leave?

Mike slapped his notebook shut and got up to leave. Only 5:35pm... but it's Friday!

A Special Friday Night

When Mike walked through the door a wall of complex aromas hit his nose. Finally, dinner with Marie. Mike dropped his briefcase and keys near the door and rushed into the kitchen. He hugged Marie with his face buried into her neck. Her scent along with the scent of the food made both his mouth and his eyes water.

"Oh, honey, I know it's been only a week but it feels like we've been separated for a month," Mike whispered into Marie's ear. "I am not complete without you. I miss holding you. I miss talking to you. I miss snuggle time!"

Marie's eyes glistened. "I love you, Mike. You'll get your feet on the ground soon and we will be back to normal. We both knew that the first few weeks would be hard. I didn't think it would be *this* hard…but we'll get through it. Now, relax and taste this Merlot."

Mike relished every moment of the spectacular dinner. How did she create a great dinner after she put in a long day at work as well? They lingered over the last drop of wine then headed for bed. Mike didn't tell Marie that his plans were to go to the office early Saturday morning to catch up. Quiet time with no other staff around would be a good time to do some serious planning.

Saturday Morning

Mike woke early and brewed a large batch of extra strong coffee. By the time Marie came to the kitchen he had downed three cups, no, maybe four. Marie hugged Mike then poured herself a cup of the deep aromatic coffee.

"Honey, I need a few hours in the office to be able to think about what's going on. I didn't want to ruin our evening by telling you about the problems, but boy, are there problems. I'm not sure what direction to take on some of these issues. I guess I just need to stare at the walls for a while and hope for inspiration. I'm sorry to leave you alone again but I will be home before dinner. How about if you make reservations at the Red Lion Inn?"

The disappointment on Marie's face was glaring. They usually spent Saturdays doing errands and chores. It didn't seem like work when they did these tasks together. It was almost fun. Marie's job as a Physician's Assistant at St Mary's Hospital was stressful and hectic. At only 34 years of age, she had established herself as a key employee in the Oncology Department. She relied on Mike's help on Saturdays to keep the house running smoothly, but more importantly, to keep their marriage running smoothly.

"I'll make reservations for 7:00 so you have some time to relax when you get home. Don't work *too* hard," Marie added, knowing that her admonishments would have no influence on Mike.

Mike sat at his desk and pulled out the letter from Don. He reread the last paragraph three times. Don's "sage" advice, as he put it. "Don't be too proud to ask for help."

"HELP!" Mike screamed at Don's picture. "I'm not proud. I need help."

Mike pulled out his notebook and added two more big issues to his list.

BIG ISSUES

1. Electronics product displaced by customer (ST Electronics) = 8% decrease in revenue ???
2. Stellar Products contract renewal = 5% risk to revenue.
3. Lupine Oil production = ?? increase in revenue.
4. Lupine Oil capital cost = $265,000 !!!!!
5. Cost of ISO 9001 and FDA approval = ??
6. Rerouting and rework of product = cost??
7. Should we be making all these base products or stop??
8. Was Don planning a layoff?
9. What to do if Sally decides to retire?
10. Is the company headed for big financial trouble?
11. Is Eric really planning to leave?
12. Can I preserve my marriage to Marie and still run the company?
13. Am I the right guy for the job?

Chapter 3: Taking a Step Back

Meeting the Coach

"Hi, Mike. It's so nice to meet you. I understand that you've taken on a huge challenge and are considering hiring a coach to help through the transition. Tell me more about what's going on." Sandy eased herself into the chair in Mike's office and leaned toward him with what could only be described as a Mona Lisa smile.

"Challenge is an understatement. My friend and mentor, Don Smith died unexpectedly of a massive heart attack. He asked me to be the interim, or maybe permanent, CEO and finish his legacy. Don meant so much to me that I really want to make him proud of me, but I'm overwhelmed. Quite honestly, last weekend I told my wife that I was going to tell Kathryn, my boss at MagTech Consulting that they should start the search for a permanent CEO because I'm just not up to it. When I met with Kathryn, she suggested that before I make that decision, I should talk to you. She gives you a five star rating and said that you have helped many clients to do the impossible. But, I'm not even sure what a coach does, so can we start there?"

Sandy's smile turned into a giggle. "First, thanks for the kind words. I have been lucky, and blessed, to work with some amazing people who really have accomplished outstanding things. But, let's be clear. They accomplished, I was on the sidelines. I am an excellent coach. They are excellent CEOs. Think of it like I'm Jason Garrett and you're Tony Romo."

"Ok. So how would it work with us, Ms. Garrett?"

"First, let me tell you what I, as your coach will do and what I will not do. I will do a lot of listening, observing and asking questions. Most of my questions will try to get you to rethink your assumptions and change the context to see new possibilities. I will reflect back to you, kind of like a mirror, so you see your actions from a different perspective. And, I will give you tough feedback, not always fun, but definitely honest and with your best interests in mind. I will suggest resources for you, such as books, articles, exercises and activities. Most important, I will ask you to commit to positive actions that you choose and I will hold you accountable for following through with those actions."

Sandy took a deep breath then continued. "I like to organize our sessions into three parts. First, I will follow up on your commitment from the previous session. Then, I'll ask you "what is the most pressing issue to talk about today?" And, finally, we will talk about the next step and your commitment for the next session."

Sandy paused and let that sink in for a few minutes, then continued. "I won't tell you what to do or how to run the company. I am a coach, not a CEO. I am not a trainer, so I will not lecture or do a lot of one-sided teaching. I am not your boss or supervisor so whatever decisions you make, I'm not here to judge you or your decisions. And, I am not a therapist, psychoanalyst or psychiatrist. I work with competent, well, healthy people to build their leadership skills and run great companies. If I believe that a client would benefit from therapy or professional counseling, I will make that recommendation."

"And, oh, by the way, a lot of times I will just be quiet so we can reflect. So, when that happens, don't feel that I'm not paying attention or that I fell asleep."

As if to demonstrate. Sandy fell silent.

"My commitment to *you* is that you are my client, not MagTech, not Square One, not the employees or even the Board. I will work with you to build your skills and always have the best interests of you and the organization in mind. I'm here for you. Yes, we will schedule meetings but I can be reached by email between meetings if you have a pressing issue. Everything we discuss is absolutely confidential. I can't stress this last part enough. What do you think?"

Sandy sat back in the chair and waited. She wasn't kidding, she could be quiet for a long time. Finally, Mike broke the silence.

"I'm in, Sandy. I owe it to myself and to Don to give this a try. When can we get started?" Sandy and Mike pulled out their calendars and scheduled weekly sessions, starting the next day and extending for the next four months. "Let's jump in hard and fast," Mike said with a self-conscious grin.

The First Session

Mike was excited about his first meeting with Sandy, but he had to admit to himself, he was also a bit skeptical. At exactly 8:55 a.m. the receptionist let him know that Sandy was waiting in the lobby.

"Nothing ventured, nothing gained," Mike said to himself as he got up to greet his coach.

After Sandy settled in and exchanged a few pleasantries, she looked at Mike with a calm resolve and asked, "Mike, what is the most important thing for us to talk about today?"

Mike took a few moments to gather his thoughts, then jumped in. "Well, Sandy, remember when I told you that I am so overwhelmed here that I think I am not being effective? I met with each of the key managers and there are too many problems looming at the door. Way too many. I'm not sure which ones to tackle first. But the worst part is that I am spending twelve hours a day doing mundane and routine tasks, so I'm exhausted and don't have the brain power left to even start on the big issues."

Mike paused and stared out the window for a moment, then continued. "No, the really worst part, is that I feel that the management team is not worried. They all seem to know their areas. Competency is not in question. It's just that they aren't concerned about the big picture. They aren't taking responsibility for their areas, not communicating with each other and dumping everything on me!"

Mike slumped into his chair with a sigh that sounded like he completely deflated, like the Snoopy balloon at the end of the Macy's Thanksgiving Day parade.

After what seemed like an eternity, Sandy finally spoke. "Tell me more about what you mean when you say they are dumping everything on you."

"Like yesterday, Sally gave me quotes from three companies for a new printer for the Admin area. She wanted me to review them and tell her which one to buy. The most expensive one was three hundred dollars, for heaven's sake. And, Jessica showed me three designs for the company Christmas card for this year and left them on my desk so I could decide. At the end of every day, Eric brings me all of the checks for signature, even the really small routine ones, like the bottled water vendor. I'm here until midnight every day trying to catch up on these tasks. But, worst of all is that they don't talk to each other. Eric will ask me what R&D expenses he should expect instead of discussing it directly with Alan. Jessica and John don't coordinate the marketing and sales efforts. John doesn't talk to Todd before committing to a shipping date when he makes a sale. They all come to me for the answers. They don't want to work as a team."

"So what I hear you saying is that the managers bring information to you and expect you to make all the decisions. Did I get that right?"

"Right. They don't want to take responsibility for any decisions."

"Why do you think they don't want to take responsibility?"

"Well, they bring every decision to me. If they wanted the responsibility, they wouldn't act that way."

"Is there another way you could interpret their actions?"

"I don't know. I just don't know. Let me think about that."

"And, you said that they don't talk to each other. You said that you think they don't want to collaborate? Why wouldn't they *want* to collaborate? I would like for you to focus on the verb 'want'. What do you think is going on?"

"I guess it's easier to depend on me to filter and pass on the information. Again, they don't want to take any responsibility."

Sandy sat quietly, then asked, "Mike, can I take off my coach hat for a minute and tell you about some definitions that may help us get to the bottom of this issue?"

"Sure, go ahead."

"I want to introduce two words, assertions and assumptions. An assertion is the description of something that can be verified by another person with an independent standard. For example, if I say that the temperature in the room is 72 degrees, you can look at the thermostat and verify if that's true or not true. Or, if I say that the company sold one hundred units of a product last month, you could look at the sales receipts to check the numbers. On the other hand, an assumption is a judgment or opinion. So, if I say, it's hot in here, you may agree or disagree, depending on your personal preferences. And if I say that sales last month didn't meet expectations, again, it's an interpretation or opinion. What's really interesting is that it's the assumptions that reflect our view of reality and determine our future actions. So, it's really important to be sure that our assumptions are grounded in assertions or facts. Does that make sense?"

"Ok, I get that. Don't jump to conclusions unless you have facts to back it up."

Sandy waved her hands around the room, pointing to the piles of folders and papers on Mike's desk. "I can see that the managers are giving you a lot of information. And, I have noticed that they line up at your door but rarely chat amongst themselves. So, when you tell me that they bring you information so you can make decisions, I think I can verify that.

I think if I spent more time watching the group dynamics, I could also verify that they don't communicate with each other very well. So, are the descriptions of these behaviors assertions or assumptions?"

Mike tapped the stack of reports on the left side of his desk and said, "Definitely, assertions."

"Agreed. Now, you said that you think they don't want responsibility, don't want to work as a team and want you to make all the decisions. What are these?"

"Probably assumptions. OK, I get it. You want me to not jump to conclusions about the 'why'. When I think I know why without having all the facts about the 'why', then I'm making an assumption. I guess I need to spend some more time observing and maybe even asking why. Can you get me started in the right direction?"

Chapter 4: L = Listen

"Mike, can I tell you about a leadership model that I think will help you?"

"Yes, please do, Sandy."

"The model is called "The L.E.A.R.N.E.D. Leader"." Sandy handed Mike a 3 by 5 inch laminated card with bold words on it.

THE L.E.A.R.N.E.D. LEADER

L = Listen

E = Examine through Appreciative Inquiry and Powerful Questions

A = Accept without judging; it is what it is

R = Reflect on what you know

N = Navigate the way forward; define success; set goals

E = Engage all the stakeholders; get input and buy-in

D = Do; take action towards the goals

"L.E.A.R.N.E.D. is an acronym for Listen, Examine, Accept without judging, Reflect, Navigate the way forward, Engage the right people, and, Do. Let's dig into the first step, Listen.

"I think to get a better handle on your assumption of the 'why' for the behaviors you're seeing, you need to listen to the managers in an active way. I call it 'WEB based listening'. W for words, E for emotions and B for body language. Wait a minute! Stop laughing! I admit I love acronyms!"

"Sorry....LEARNED Leader, WEB based listening, I'm going to need a dictionary!"

"You have a particularly difficult challenge when it comes to hearing what the managers are saying. Most of us listen with only a small portion of our brains. We are so busy formulating our responses, thinking about our interpretation of what is being said and managing distractions, that much of what is being said is simply missed. Your first task will be to learn to really listen and focus on what is being said. But, you have to learn a second layer of listening. If your managers like you, they won't want to disappoint you. They want to keep their jobs. They are not sure who you are and how you will react. They don't know your leadership and management style. So, I suspect that they are also unintentionally putting a spin on what they say. You have to unspin it. That's why you need to focus, not only on the words, but pay attention to the body language, the tone of voice, facial expressions, intonations and delve into the emotions behind the words. When you really hear what is being said then your interpretation of the 'why' will be more accurate and your actions based on the interpretation will be solid."

"I get it. Can we practice? I would like to discuss something I'm 'hearing'?"

"Great. Let's process it. First, tell me the words you hear, without interpretation."

"Well, my first day here, at the end of the all-company meeting to describe the transition, all of the employees shook my hand and several of them addressed me as 'Boss'. I thought they were just being encouraging...."

"Wait," Sally interrupted, "no interpretation, just the words."

"Sorry, but thanks. I see how quickly I assign a 'why' to the words. This will be hard to stop. Anyway, most of the managers continue to call me 'Boss', as in 'thanks, Boss' or 'you got it, Boss' or 'what's up, Boss'. At first, I corrected them and told them to call me Mike. Now, I just let it go. But, I have to admit it bothers me."

"So, you hear the word 'Boss' being used to address you instead of your name. What have you noticed about the tone of voice and body language that's used when the managers call you 'Boss'?"

"Jen Brown is Director of Quality and she has been with the company for about three years. She usually smiles, but doesn't look at me. John Black, Director of Sales, has been with the company a long time, over ten years. It seems that he usually says it as he's walking away from me, kind of an over-the-shoulder throw-away. Todd Wall, Director of Operations has a lot of seniority, about twenty years, and he knows me from my years as a consultant to the company. Now that I'm thinking about it, I can almost picture a question mark after the word 'Boss' when he says it. His voice actually goes up a little bit at the end of the word. With Alan Atkins, Director of R&D, the tone is a bit dismissive, as if he can't be bothered remembering my name. I almost expect him to call me pal or kiddo. Eric Miller, Director of Finance, well, there's some sarcasm there. He has been with the company five years and it's pretty obvious to him that I'm no expert in finance. I wondered why Don didn't choose him to be the interim CEO. Maybe he's wondering the same thing. Sally Jones, head of HR, worked her way up from secretary over twenty years ago. She calls me 'Mr. Townsend' and it always has an official sound to it. And, Jessica White, another relatively new person, three years with the company....humph....she doesn't use anything, not 'Boss', not 'Mike'.....I didn't notice that until just now."

"What I hear you say is that the way the managers address you varies but the common thread is that nobody calls you 'Mike' even though you have encouraged them to do so. Did I capture that?"

"Yeah. Wow, I didn't put that together until just now."

"Great observations, Mike. I noticed you reflected on body language, tone, facial expressions and cadence. Now, let's throw in some of the emotions. What emotions are you 'hearing' from the managers? And, what emotions are you feeling when you hear what they say? Let's make two lists."

Mike pulled out a blank paper, folded it in half and wrote on one side "emotions I am hearing" and on the other, "emotions I am feeling".

"OK, the emotions I think I am hearing are: uncertainty, respect, I mean respect for the position, not necessarily for me personally, distrust, fear, anger, resentment, passivity, dismissiveness, disrespect, and, unconnectedness, if that's a real word.

"And, how does it make me feel? Not good. I would say: hurt, scared, alone, burdened, carrying the weight of the world, disrespected, walled-out, frustrated, and, like they may be waiting for me to fail."

Sandy sat very quietly. It seemed like an eternity. Then in a very quiet and calm voice, she asked, "What does all this tell you?"

Mike met her eyes and said, "They don't know me and they don't trust me as a leader." Mike sank back in his chair as if his own words knocked the wind out of him.

"Congratulations, Mike! You have just seen the power of really listening. You learned a lot from hearing, really hearing, just one word, just a salutation. Keep listening. I would like you to think about how to build trust in a team. I'm going to email you some 'homework' to do.

What Just Happened?

Mike slumped back in his chair. An hour. Sandy was in his office for just one hour. How could he be so drained and energized at the same time? Mike pulled out a pen and his notebook and summarized what Sandy had said about assertions and assumptions. Assertions = factual data I can verify. Assumptions = subjective judgments or conclusions I make.

He thought about what had happened during the meeting. He assumed a coach would tell him what to do. Sandy didn't *tell* him anything. She asked him questions and things got clearer. He had an "Ah-Ha" moment. Mike also realized that he felt that he could tell her anything and she would not judge him. He felt safe and comfortable with her. "How did she do that in our first meeting and in just one hour?" Mike asked himself.

Email from Sandy

To: Mike Townsend

From: Sandy Bishop

Subject: Your Listening Assignment

Hi, Mike:

Thanks for a very productive first session. I warned you that I would give you assignments and here is your first one on listening. I am attaching some rules for active listening. Read them and think about ways that you can implement each rule. Spend a little time with them.

Next I'm asking you to get the movie Before Sunset (2004) directed by Richard Linklater. It is one of a trilogy of films about the lives of two people played by Ethan Hawke and Julie Delpy. Each film is just one long conversation. So for the first part of the exercise, turn off the video and listen to ten minutes of the film. Stop the film and describe the characters and the conversation that they had. Did they really listen to each other? What emotions did you hear? Did they break any of the listening rules? What was the effect when they did? What is your interpretation of their relationship? How do you feel about the characters?

Then stop the film and switch to the video with the audio muted. For the next ten minutes watch the film without listening to the words. What emotions are you seeing? What is the body language telling you? Did they break any of the listening rules? What was the effect when they did? Now what is your interpretation of their relationship? How did it change? How do you feel about the characters now?

Finally, go back to the beginning and watch the same twenty minutes of the film with both the audio and video. What did you miss compared to when you saw only the video or only heard the words? And finally, what did you learn from the exercise? We'll talk about it in our next session. See you next week.

The Do and Don't Rules for Active Listening

<u>**Do**</u>

1. **Keep eye contact**
2. **Give acknowledgements that you are listening by nodding, saying yes, ok or ah ha**
3. **Paraphrase back what you heard**
4. **Name an emotion you heard such as, "you sound upset" or "sounds like that made you happy"**
5. **Mirror back a phrase as a question. "He left yesterday?"**
6. **Put your own emotions on the shelf**
7. **Ignore distractions**
8. **Use open body language, relaxed arms, leaning in towards the person**
9. **Stop talking**
10. **Be patient**
11. **Pay attention to the tone**
12. **Watch body language and non-verbal signals**
13. **Be respectful**
14. **Be aware of what the person is not saying as well as what they are saying**
15. **Note your emotions as you listen but do not react emotionally**
16. **Think about why the person is telling you this. If you're not sure, ask why**

The Do and Don't Rules for Active Listening

Don't

1. Multitask
2. Get distracted
3. Assume you know what the person is going to say
4. Start thinking of a response or answer while the person is talking
5. Interrupt
6. Judge the information or the person
7. Correct the person
8. Become defensive
9. Jump to conclusions or finish the person's sentences
10. Show signs of impatience, fiddle with stuff, glance at the clock

Marie Helps With the Homework

Friday evening Mike got home just as Marie was setting the table for dinner. It smelled great. In his hand was the DVD of the movie Before Sunset.

"Hi Honey, TGIF," Mike said as he enveloped Marie in a big hug. "Remember I told you about Sandy's email? Well, I managed to borrow a copy of the movie and was hoping you would help me with my homework."

"Actually it sounds like fun. And, I think I'll learn something useful as well."

As soon as the dishes were cleared, Mike popped in the DVD and gave Marie copies of the rules for active listening. They settled into the couch with pens and paper for taking notes.

After the first ten minutes of listening to the movie without seeing the characters, Marie and Mike sighed in unison. This was harder than they thought. Following ten minutes of watching the movie without the audio, they looked at each other and laughed.

"Her body language was very provocative."

"His body language was in and out, like he was reaching toward her then pulling back, a human yo-yo."

"They kept eye contact but did not stare."

"They occasionally touched with a brief grazing touch."

"They both were focused on communicating."

"Sometimes she assumed what he was going to say and then she was wrong."

"The conversation spun into so many directions but there was always a thread."

"Her accent is so cute."

Mike and Marie continued for about thirty minutes, comparing notes and sharing observations. Then it became personal.

"Don't take this the wrong way, Mike, but sometimes you violate rule 10. You check your phone, look at the clock, fiddle with your pen, so that I feel like you want me to hurry up and stop talking."

"I appreciate your honesty, Marie. After reading the rules, I realized that I violate more than one. This has been a great exercise in self-awareness. Thank you for doing this with me."

"I learned a lot too," said Marie as she snuggled into Mike's arms. "Now, let's just watch the whole movie."

The Coaching Continues

The week flew by. Late nights. Missed dinners. Data gathering. Solving a million problems. Making a billion little decisions. Mike realized just how much he was looking forward to his conversation with Sandy.

As soon as Sandy settled in she asked, "So, did you do your homework?"

"I did. And, I don't know if this is cheating but I asked my wife, Marie, to do it along with me. It was an eye –opener. We learned a lot from the exercise but also from our conversations about the exercise. I think you could use this as a marriage counseling technique."

"Listening is key to good relationships, both business and personal. I'm glad you and Marie had fun. Tell me about your conclusions."

"Well, I found that when I heard only the words I judged the characters more harshly. I missed the depth of the relationship that was developing. But when I only watched them, I interpreted the relationship in a more physical way. Together I had a more balanced view of the characters. I liked them. I could relate more. Most important, the exercise made me realize the importance of what you call 'WEB-based listening'. I heard the words, paid attention to the emotions and watched the body language."

"What will you do differently now?" Sandy asked.

"Marie pointed out that I fidget when I'm listening, which probably sends out the message that I'm not paying attention or in a hurry. I will stop that. When I'm listening my brain is formulating questions, conclusions and I jump ahead. I'm thinking of solutions before I hear the whole problem. I'm going to focus on being present in the conversation. And, finally, I think I interrupt a lot. Marie suggested that I count to five before saying anything so that I give the other person a chance to finish before I jump in. I like her suggestion. I've been practicing these techniques but I still have a long way to go."

"All great ways to improve your listening skills. At our next session, I'd like you to tell me how that worked for you. Now, what is most important to talk about today?"

Chapter 5: E = Examine

Mike jumped right in. He had anticipated Sandy's question and after much thought, he concluded that he needed to be able to dig deeper in order to understand the situation at Square One.

"Remember when I told you that I was feeling overwhelmed with the weight of the entire company on my shoulders. Well, it hasn't gotten any better. The treadmill is going at a faster and faster pace. As I mentioned, all week I've been much more focused on practicing active listening with the team and I think I have a much better understanding of the issues we're facing. But it feels like there are things that they're not telling me. Maybe it's related to our discussion last week about trust. I'm not sure. What do I do?"

Sandy's smile broadened. "What a setup. I could not have asked for a better introduction to the next section of The L.E.A.R.N.E.D. Leader."

Sandy pulled out her laminated card. "Examine through Appreciative Inquiry and Powerful Questions. You get more information by asking questions, the *right* questions. First, some definitions. "Appreciative Inquiry" is the use of questions to determine the best of a situation so that you can determine a positive future state. Typically, we tend to focus on the problems, the "what's wrong here" attitude. "Appreciative Inquiry" challenges us to find out "what's right here", what is successful, what worked in the past, what has future promise. Think of it as a model to accentuate the positive. After we understand what's the best, then we ask the question 'what would the organization look like if the best became the norm rather than the exception?'. I suspect that as you met your team you've been asking questions that have focused on problems. When that happens, people clam up, get defensive, hide information and go into the self-preservation mode. Especially with the new boss in town. When you ask about what's working well, people open up, get excited, get more engaged and get energized."

"I feel like an idiot," said Mike. "I have been focused on the problems. I've been digging into what's wrong. I put my 'I can solve anything hat' firmly on my head and plowed in. I suspect there are a lot of bruised toes…and egos here. What can I do to turn this around?"

Sandy looked at Mike with a gentle smile. "Before we get into that, I need to give you one more definition. 'Powerful Questions'. Did you ever hear the advice that lawyers give each other? Never ask a question if you don't know the answer. That advice may work in a court room but in leadership it is absolutely the wrong way to go. Ask questions that are open ended, that bring clarity, are challenging, and most important, that expand learning and give a fresh perspective."

"I think I get it but it sounds like it would be hard to be so upbeat and ignore the problems," Mike said with a perplexed look on his face.

"It's easier than you think," said Sandy. "It's a mindset. Maybe if I give you an example, you'll see the power of this approach. One of my client companies was in the environmental science field. They were having a problem with high turnover of employees and since training costs were high, their labor costs were out of line and getting worse. The pattern was that the company would hire new college graduates, then in two to three years the employees would be recruited by pharmaceutical companies and leave for higher pay. My coachee, Mary, was head of human resources and was tasked to solve the problem. She had initiated a program of exit interviews and performance reviews. The data seemed to indicate that the employees were not dissatisfied, and, in fact were really sad to leave, but the higher pay was too tempting. The employees also felt that after two or three years of focused learning they deserved more responsibility and money. They wanted to be recognized for their efforts and the offers from pharmaceutical companies were flattering. The company could not compete with the higher salaries offered in the pharmaceutical industry so Mary seemed resigned to tell her boss that they would just have to live with the high costs and high employee turnover rate."

"I can relate to that situation," said Mike, "I've seen it before."

"After we talked about 'Powerful Questions' and 'Appreciative Inquiry', I challenged Mary to look at the issue again. She sought out those employees who stayed longer than three years and asked them why they stayed. Then she asked employees with one or two years in the company what they wanted to happen in their careers and what the company was doing right. She even went out on a limb and called three individuals who had left the company for the pharmaceutical positions. She used open ended questions and compiled the information. The results were surprising. The new college graduates with no experience had difficulty finding jobs so they were extremely grateful when they were given an opportunity. They believed in the mission of the company and felt that their work had impact on the customers and on the environment. They liked the team and the work. The company's training program was so valuable that pharmaceutical firms were like vultures, picking off the trained staff. Those that stayed were happy. Another interesting thing she found out was that the three employees that left were disappointed in the work in their new jobs and one even asked if he could come back."

"OK, I'm on the edge of my seat. What did they do?"

"They listed all the things they were doing right, great training, giving the kids a chance, safe and clean facilities, meaningful work, engaged employees, and excellent management. They redesigned the employment structure for new college graduates, giving them a three year apprenticeship. They reduced the pay for the first three years while the training was very intensive. They gave each employee a personalized training program so they could measure their progress but also take a longer term view of their careers at the company. They assigned a mentor to each new hire. At the end of the three years the employee was either terminated or promoted to a permanent position at a significantly higher pay. At that point the employee was also put in training for a supervisory role or for additional technical training depending upon whether the individual wanted to go into management or stay in a technical track. These people also became involved in the training and mentoring of the new staff. The turnover dropped dramatically and the overall labor costs decreased even more dramatically. Mary credits the entire new structure to looking at what they did right and building on it."

Mike sat back and let it sink in. "You're right. That example is a real eye opener, a very creative solution."

"So, Mike, let's get back to your situation. You said that you think you understand many of the issues here but that there are some things that you feel the staff is not telling you. Is there another way you could interpret what you are experiencing?"

"I've been so focused on the problems that I know I've missed lots of good things that are happening. I'm the new guy and the staff doesn't know me and probably doesn't trust me so they're not sure how much of their concerns to share. I suspect that they're worried about their jobs and whether or not I'll find a scapegoat to blame for the problems. I guess a different way to interpret what I'm experiencing is that I'm not asking the right questions and I don't have the right perspective. Maybe I'm still acting like a consultant, digging into the problem and handing out solutions. Maybe I'm not acting like part of the team!" Mike's voice was almost a whisper as reality set in.

"At the beginning of this meeting I was going to show you my list of Big Issues and ask for help. I changed my mind. I want to think about how to create the list of Big Pluses that I can develop to show you next time. Can we talk about how I can do that?"

"Absolutely, Mike. What types of questions can you ask your staff to get a different view of what's going on?"

Mike pulled out his tablet and wrote as fast as he spoke.

1. How did the company (or your department) get to this point?
2. What are the best parts of your department and your job?
3. What things are you most proud of?
4. What's the opportunity here?
5. What challenges have you overcome in the past?
6. What did you do to succeed?

7. What's your dream for your department, for the company, for yourself?
8. What is necessary for us to get to your dream?
9. What are the dreams of others in the company?
10. If anything were possible, what would you like to see happen here?
11. What role would you like to play in the company going forward?
12. What scares the competition?
13. What delights the customers?
14. What would you like me to do to help?

After Mike filled up one and a half pages of questions, Sandy said, "You've got the concept but I'd like you to notice the format of your questions."

Mike studied the list then slowly said, "Almost every question starts with the word 'what'."

"Good observation. I'd like to give you an example to reinforce that. You told me about Marie's skill in the kitchen. Suppose you came home from work and she asked you if you want spaghetti for dinner. How would you respond?"

"I guess I would say yes or no."

"But, then what?"

"I would wonder if she had her heart set on spaghetti and if I'm now in trouble or would she be eating spaghetti and I would have an empty plate," said Mike with a grin.

"So by asking a question that has a yes or no response, the response not only is limited, but the person may try to give you the response they think you want."

"OK."

"What if she asked if you want spaghetti or chicken fingers?"

"Not much better. I'd still try to find out what she had in mind."

Sandy laughed. "That kind of question is what I call controlled empowerment. I use it with my daughter. It gives her power over choices but in a limited range and I set the range. She is not a big fan of vegetables so last night I asked her if she wanted broccoli or carrots. I didn't give her the choice of skipping vegetables."

"Interesting," said Mike. "I think I fell for that one. John came to me with a question about pricing for a contract renewal for a key customer. He asked me if he should offer a higher price, the same price or a lower price."

"The vegetable trap," Marie said. "How did you react to the question?"

"I have to admit that my brain immediately went to those three solutions. I didn't think of other options. And, I tried to figure out what he was suggesting by the order of the options."

"Great observations. Let's go back to the dinner example. What if Marie told you that she had been to the grocery store and bought fresh chicken, lean ground beef, crisp lettuce, bright red tomatoes, and a variety of sweet peppers, then asked you what would tickle your palate."

"I would start throwing out suggestions, like tacos, chicken marsala, and pasta primavera."

"What was different in the questions and your answers?"

"She set the parameters by describing the ingredients in tantalizing ways. Then, the 'what' question made me think creatively. And, finally, the form of the question made me feel like part of the decision and I wouldn't worry what she had in mind."

"Excellent, Mike, now how could John have posed the question to get a similar response from you?"

"If he had described the situation then asked about a strategy for future pricing, I would have thought more broadly, suggested more options and been more creative. I think I would have put his question into the perspective of the whole company and our strategy instead of thinking of it as an isolated issue."

"So as you think of digging deeper, set the stage in a positive fashion, then start every question with the word 'what'. I just let you in on a secret coaching trick. Start every question with the word 'what'." Sandy smiled as she put her fingers to her lips pretending to lock them and throw away the key.

"Mike, as we end this session, I would like to circle back to something you said earlier. You said that maybe you were acting like a consultant not a member of the team. I would like you to think about that. What could you do to be perceived as a member of the team?"

What?

After Sandy left, Mike picked up the tablet and reworked the questions until he felt that he had a good list of ways to open positive conversations. Then he pulled out his notebook and started a new section with the header BIG PLUSES. Mike felt that he already knew some of the Big Pluses so he started the list.

BIG PLUSES
1. Loyal customers – need to get a better understanding of why they are loyal.
2. Efficient manufacturing
3. Good reputation in the industry – but why?
4. Engaged and dedicated staff
5. Supportive Board of Directors

Then Mike decided to start a third section in the notebook. He thought for a long while then wrote the header and the questions that were heavy on his mind.

Mike
1. Am I the right guy for the job?
2. Do I want to be the President long term?
3. What can I do to gain the trust of the team?
4. What can I do so that I am perceived as a member of the team and not as a consultant?

Mike stared at the list for a long while then shook his head. Whoa, I violated Sandy's advice already, Mike thought. Only two of my questions begin with the word "what" and the first two get a yes or no answer. This needs work.

Mike took the first question and wrote down other ways to ask it that began with the word "what". "I'll worry about the grammar later, but I need to brainstorm these questions, he muttered."

What would I be if I was the right guy?

What would I look like if I was the right guy?

What would I look like if I'm not the right guy?

What would prevent me from being the right guy?

What do I have that would make me the right guy?

What would it take for me to be the right guy?

What would I have to give up in order to be the right guy?

What would I have to change in order to be the right guy?

Well, that's a start, Mike thought as he moved on to the second question.

What would make me want to be the President for the long term?

What would make me not want to be President for the long term?

"That one was a lot easier to rewrite but probably not much easier to answer," said Mike as he leaned back in his chair. "Enough questions for now. I need to work on getting some answers."

The First Team Meeting – First Thing Monday Morning

"Good Morning, everyone. I hope you had a good weekend and are ready to jump into a challenging week," Mike said as he sat in the chair at the head of the conference table. "Thanks for being prompt. I've been spending a lot of time with each of you and I think this is the right time to begin having weekly staff meetings. My goal is to improve communication among all of you so that I am not the information funnel."

"Look, Boss, I'm on the road a lot so I don't think I can make many of these meetings," said John, interrupting with more than a bit of impatience already in his voice.

"What time are you planning on scheduling the meetings?" Todd was not smiling as he asked his question. "Manufacturing starts at 7:00 and if the meetings are always at 8:00 then I won't be on the production floor. This is when most of the process emergencies happen so I'll probably have to leave the meetings to deal with the emergencies."

"Lots of holidays fall on a Monday so you need to think about that as well," said Sally.

"This is a small company. Do you really think we need to meet every week?" Alan was shifting restlessly in his seat.

"You all have made good points," said Mike as he looked around the table. None of the faces were smiling back at him. "But I disagree with you, Alan. This is no longer a small company. And, if we're lucky…and smart…it'll get even bigger. As I met with each of you I observed that you each gave me information but it appeared that you don't share information with each other as much as you could. I want these staff meetings to facilitate that. The company is facing some major decisions and has some interesting opportunities that could open up. I want us to work on these as a team. Yes, I said *us*. Let me say it again, *US*. I know that Don founded this company and that his style was different than mine. But I want this team to work as a team. I believe that together we can build this company to realize not only Don's dream, but our own dreams as well."

Mike turned to Eric and then said to the team, "Eric used the image of a spoke and wheel. He said that Don was the hub of the wheel and that all of you were spokes who interacted with Don but not with each other. I heard frustration about this from some of the rest of you as well. You're all smart, dedicated experts in your specialties. I believe that if we work as a team we have a much better chance of succeeding."

"Look, Boss, don't blame me for speaking my mind," said Eric.

Mike was silent. One one thousand, two one thousand, three one thousand, four one thousand, five one thousand. Marie's five seconds before you respond rule. "Not at all Eric. I'm grateful that you spoke out. You had the courage to say something that I was beginning to discover. I also think that there's been an elephant in the room. That elephant has the words 'THE NEW GUY' written on it. Is the new guy going to run this place like Don did? Will the new guy change things? Is the new guy good enough? Who will the new guy like? Who will the new guy get rid of? What's the new guy's agenda? Is the new guy going to stay or is he a flash in the pan? What's the next new guy going to do?"

That got their attention. The staff leaned forward in their seats.

"And another thing," Mike continued. "Stop calling me Boss. My name is Mike. Not Boss. Not Mr. Townsend. Just Mike. Is that OK with everyone?"

Heads nodded in agreement. Now he really had their attention.

"And lastly, I'm not afraid of leading the team. I'm prepared to put my all into this company. I will lead. I will coordinate. I will be responsible to the Board. But I expect each of you to be leaders as well. Understood?"

"Today's meeting will be a short one. I just want to get a commitment from each of you to make these meetings a priority on your calendars and more importantly, a priority in your heads. So, let's agree to a time and day for the meetings and an overall agenda or format."

The next thirty minutes were spent discussing a schedule and marking calendars with a recurring event for every Wednesday morning from 8:00 to 9:30 with a soft reserve on the 9:30 to 10:00 slot in case the meeting went a bit long. The general agenda would follow a format with each team member giving a five minute update of progress in their areas then an in-depth discussion of the topic of the day. The meeting would close with an action plan and commitments from each Manager to focus on the goals for the week.

"I know our first meeting on Wednesday is only two days away but I think it's important to set the stage," said Mike as he handed each person a stapled set of papers. The staff quickly flipped through the papers and looked at him in confusion. Each page had the name of one of the team members and nothing else.

"I've given each of you a set of papers with names on the top of blank sheets of paper. Between now and Wednesday morning I want you to fill in the pages without discussing them with each other. First go to the page with your own name on it. Write down all of your job responsibilities. Then fill in the sheets with the other names describing that person's responsibilities as clearly as you understand them. Be sure to write only what you believe the other person's responsibilities to be, don't ask anyone for clarification. Bring the sheets to the meeting on Wednesday. We will unstaple the pages and hand the sheets to the person whose name is on top. I'll give you some time to read them all. This will tell you what others think you do or don't know that you do. Then each person will read to the group what they think they are responsible for. Then we'll talk about gaps, those tasks that nobody seems to be responsible for and overlaps, those tasks that more than one person seems to be responsible for. I think the discussion will be interesting. Now, let's get to work."

"Thanks, Mike," said Todd as the group filed out of the conference room. "This is a step in the right direction."

The nods and smiles on all of the faces were thanks enough for Mike.

Chapter 6: A = Accept

"Well, Mike, you're smiling more than last week. I can't wait to hear what's been happening." Sandy's perky voice and bright red sweater seemed to lighten the room.

"I think I am making progress, especially with sorting out some of my questions. Our last session was really valuable. I spent a lot of time rewriting my questions. Then I was very careful to use the open-ended 'what' questions to start every conversation. I experienced a shift in attitude with most of the staff. They shared more information and some of the tension seems to be easing. And, they're calling me Mike instead of Boss."

Mike shared with Sandy the details of his first staff meeting and the work that he planned to do with the team at the meeting on Wednesday.

"I'm looking forward to the meeting. But, I'm also a bit worried. I think they'll take it seriously but I don't want finger pointing or excuses."

"Ah," said Sandy, "let's talk about the 'A' in the L.E.A.R.N.E.D. Leader, 'Accept'. To accept without judging is to listen mindfully and to be present without putting your own opinions into what you hear. What they say is a description of how it is. Not how you would like it to be or even how they would like it to be. Just what is. This meeting will tell you what your starting point is. If you don't understand your starting point, then your plans to move forward may not be grounded in reality. This is a great opportunity."

"I realize what's at stake and I don't want to blow it."

"What can you do to ensure that the meeting will be a success?"

"I guess the major responsibility falls on my shoulders. I need to accept without judging. But more important, I need to not just be an example of accepting without judging but be the enforcer of the policy as well. I need to guard the openness."

"What can you do to keep your mind in an accepting zone?"

"I think I need to write the ground rules on the board and talk about them at the beginning of the meeting."

"What are those ground rules?"

"Here are my thoughts. I'd like to get a small basket that I put on the table and ask everyone to put their egos in the basket for the duration of the meeting. Then, I'll talk about Appreciative Inquiry and tell them that after someone speaks we need to ask open-ended, clarifying questions to get a better understanding of what they are saying. If someone violates the rules, I'll put the basket in front of that person and shake it."

"Using a symbol, like the basket, is a good reminder of the rules in a light-hearted way. What else can you do?"

"I can write some example questions on the board. And, I can be sure to praise someone who asks good questions. I think I should also write on the board our goal for the meeting, which is to get a clear understanding of all roles so I can ask if a particular discussion is helping us reach that goal."

"How will you know if it's working?"

"If we keep arrows and spears to a minimum, if I deflect the arrows as soon as possible and if we reach our goal then I'll feel good about the meeting.

"What can you do to keep the meeting on track?"

"I think that every fifteen minutes, I'll do a silent status check. I'll ask myself if there is something I can do better. If I think we need to review the rules or take a break, I'll do that. After thirty minutes, I'll give everyone a break and ask if they are OK with the progress we're making or if we need to adjust the approach."

"And, what can get in your way?"

"If I am not vigilant in keeping the rules then it could fall apart or, if they don't believe me when I tell them that they won't be judged."

"Sounds like you need to create a safe environment. What else can you do to make them feel safe?"

"I'll tell them it's safe. Even better, I'll tell them it's OK to remind me or the entire room of the rules and the goal. I'll make all of us guardians of openness. I'll tell them that it is the responsibility of all of us to guard the openness. Then, when we start reading our lists of responsibilities, I'll go first! I'll read my sheet first. I'll let them see me as a member of the team, vulnerable and working toward the solution. I'll show them that I don't have an answer in my head that I want them to find but that we will find the answer together. That's it...I'll go first!"

That's what *you* do?

Wednesday morning the team was greeted by the smell of fresh, strong coffee and cinnamon buns when they entered the conference room. Mike had already written the rules and goals on the whiteboard.

GOALS FOR TODAY
1. **Clear understanding of the responsibilities of each member of the team.**
2. **Identify any gaps**
3. **Identify any unwanted overlaps**
4. **Identify opportunities**

RULES FOR THE MEETING
1. **Be honest and open**
2. **Put your ego in the basket**
3. **No judging**
4. **No finger pointing or blaming**
5. **Use Appreciative Inquiry to ask open ended positive questions**
6. **No interruptions, no cell phones, text messages, emails, no distractions unless it is a safety matter**
7. **Be respectful of everyone's time and share the floor**
8. **Be part of the solution**

Mike reviewed the rules and the goals for the meeting. He held up a twelve inch diameter basket that he took from his kitchen that morning. He shook the basket and said, "Please put your egos into this basket and pick them up at the end of the meeting." When the laughs subsided he said, "And I'm asking that we all commit to the rules and if anybody slips, then I'm counting on the rest of you to slide the basket in front of that person and give it a good shake. That goes for me as well. If you see me violate a rule, don't hesitate to call me on it. Now, let's get started."

Each person unstapled their sheets and passed them to the person whose name was on the top of the page. Only an occasional slurp of coffee broke the silence for the next twenty minutes.

"OK," said Mike. "I'll go first. I'm going to read how I originally described my responsibilities then, I'll describe what I learned from the team. After that, we'll go around the room clockwise. Let's hold questions until everyone has had a chance to speak."

As each person took their turn, the rest of the team gave respectful attention. The basket was pushed across the table only two times.

"Wow, I'm so impressed," said Mike. Murmurs from around the table emphasized that the rest of the team shared his response. "Let's take a bio break then open it up for questions and discussions about gaps and overlaps. Please be back in ten minutes."

In less than ten minutes the team reassembled with more coffee and pastries in hand.

"Impressions, thoughts, questions?" said Mike.

"I learned more about how the company works in the past hour than I did in my three years here," said Alan. "And, I have a much better idea of how my R & D projects fit into the organization."

"Now I know where to get information that I need for my marketing campaigns and planning without bothering you, Mike," said Jessica. "Sorry, Eric and Todd, but you're going to be seeing a lot more of me."

"I felt like I was a Quality island and that my job was like Pluto, not quite a planet or equal to the others," said Jennifer. "Now I can see so many ties to the other groups. Thanks, guys. I think I'm a real planet now."

"I've been in operations for so long I started to think only about operations," said Todd. "This made me realize that I'm just a planet, not the sun. Thanks for the great analogy and the reality check, Jennifer."

"And, I saw the company in numbers, just numbers," said Eric. "As everyone spoke, it put life into the numbers. I have a much better understanding of why we're committing resources to certain areas. I promise I'll stop being such a pain in your butts about those purchase orders. But I think I also realized that I can provide some special financial reports and data to each of you that will help you do your jobs better. I'd like to meet with each of you to see how I can help."

Sally's eyes filled with tears. "I don't mean to look like a sappy old woman but I was transported back in time. You all know that I was with Don from the beginning. In the early years we all knew what every person in the company was doing every day. This meeting would have been irrelevant. I think that through the years I forgot the importance of collaboration and communication. I got so jaded that I started seeing the employees as just another person on the HR roles, just another person who needed to be enrolled in the insurance policies, and just another piece of paper to be filed. I forgot how important you all are. We are a company because of the employees. I feel like a real jerk." Immediately, Todd and Jennifer reached out to hug Sally while the rest of the team whispered encouragements.

The team looked at John. After what seemed like a long silence, John looked up from his sheets. "I don't know how this will help me sell our products. I see that the company is moving in some new directions that I didn't quite understand. So, I guess this has been helpful in that." John did not try to hide his discomfort.

Mike stood. "First, I want to thank all of you for sharing in such an open and supportive manner. I'm impressed that we only pushed the basket two times. What I learned is that there are lots of ways we can improve the way we do things. I'm seeing curiosity and appreciation of each other's roles in the company. I'm hearing interest and intent to collaborate. For me, this has been a great session. Thank you. Now, another quick bio break and let's review our goals."

In less than five minutes the group came back ready to tackle the review of the goals. "I think we hit goal number #1 completely," said Mike. "What about goal #2, what gaps did we identify?"

"This discussion made me realize that we had become isolated from each other, but now I have to ask if we have become just as isolated from our customers?" After Todd posed the question, most of the heads nodded in agreement.

"I think you hit the nail on the head with that one," said Jessica, "especially as we're looking to develop new products. But I'm going to push even farther and ask if we've become isolated from our competitors and suppliers as well."

"Are we ignoring the other solar systems?" Jennifer said. "Maybe I'm pushing the analogy too far, but I think you know what I mean."

Mike stood and wrote on the whiteboard.

Our major gaps are:
1. **Clear understanding of the needs and wants of our current and future customers**
2. **Identify ways to optimize opportunities with competitors and suppliers**

"I think that captures it, Mike, thank you," said Todd. "I don't know if I should be really scared or excited about the possibilities that this opens up."

"Probably both," said Eric. "I'm having the same reaction in my gut."

"Now, goal #3. Do we have any unwanted overlaps?"

After a few minutes, Alan spoke out. "I noticed that many of us overlapped with you, Mike, and not with each other. I think I'm going to invoke the open and honest rule when I say this, but I've felt that I don't make any decisions or recommendations on R&D projects. I only prepare reports. That makes me feel that I could be replaced by a great Google search."

Jessica's head nodded in agreement. "I think I could do so much more than I have been if I could make recommendations instead of just giving facts. And, I'd feel like I had more at stake."

"Boy, I agree with you on that," said Eric. "If you follow the trail of paper that accompanies a purchase of supplies it gets to the point of being ridiculous. Mike, I know that these systems were in place when you got here so I am not pointing fingers. But can we rethink some of these systems?"

"Alan, Jessica, Eric, thank you," said Mike. "I agree wholeheartedly. Since I came on board, I have spent so much of my time doing tasks that I should be delegating that I haven't had the time or energy to figure out how to move the company forward. And, in the open and honest category, I thought that's the way you wanted it. I should have realized that maybe this is the way it evolved and it's time to realign. We should rethink these systems and get a better balance between responsibility and authority." Mike wrote on the whiteboard.

Our major overlaps are:
   1. **Aligning authority so it matches responsibility**
   2. **Redesigning systems to maximize efficiency without giving up quality and control**

"I don't know about the rest of you, but I'm exhausted," said Mike. "We've accomplished a lot. I'm going to ask that we put goal #4 on our agenda for next week and give ourselves some time to think about our gaps and overlaps. Thanks for a great session."

After a long day

It was after 8:00 pm when Mike finally walked through his front door and tossed his keys on the hall table.

"You look exhausted," said Marie. "But, at least you're home before midnight. Tell me about your day."

Mike reached for the glass of Cabernet that Marie handed him and let out a huge sigh. "It was a landmark day. I think almost everyone felt a shift today during the team meeting. My efforts to build a safe place to express ideas seemed to work. I heard a lot of things I didn't expect to hear, some were right in line with my thinking and some knocked my socks off. My brain is overflowing with ideas, worries and possibilities."

"Start from the beginning. Tell me everything."

In between bites of the chicken Caesar salad Mike told Marie the details of the meeting. "Thanks for listening to me, Marie. Telling you the details seems to make it all clearer to me. I don't know what I would do without you. I walked out of the meeting with my head spinning. I had spent much of the day shifting from worry to excitement. I was almost paralyzed by the swirling thoughts. You helped me to begin to put order to my ideas."

"I'm glad I could help," said Marie, as she cleaned up the dishes. "Now, let's both get some sleep."

Debrief with the Coach

Mike was anxious to tell Sandy about the outcome of the meeting. He summarized the process he had set up for building a safe space. Then he told her of the conversations and gave her a copy of the gaps and overlaps list that they had developed. Without a word, Sandy took the two lists and read them. Then she got up from her chair and put the lists on the floor beside Mike's desk.

"I'm impressed, Mike. It sounds like you accomplished a lot in your meeting. What emotions are you feeling?"

"I feel like a swirl of emotions. Excited, scared, worried, panicked, happy, satisfied, proud, terrified. Does that cover the entire range of human emotions? I seem to be swinging from idea to idea and worry to worry. Yes, we made great progress, but, where do we go from here? And, can the team accomplish it? And, the question of whether or not I'm the right guy for the job is still on my mind."

"I'm going to ask you to step back from the details and the outcome of the meeting. What is your overall feeling about the team at this point?"

"Interesting question, Sandy. Do you remember at one of our early sessions I told you that I thought that the team did not want to take responsibility for their jobs but that they wanted to just push the responsibilities onto me? I was doing a lot of day to day tasks that I thought they could do but they were just dumping them on me. You asked me if that was an assumption or an assertion."

"I do remember that conversation. So what do you think now?"

"It was definitely an assumption. I realize now that they were working within the systems that had evolved in the company. I was assuming a motivation and I was wrong. I misjudged them. I think that the biggest revelation of the meeting is that I don't have to carry all the weight on my shoulders. I can distribute some of the weight to the team to carry and some of the weight we can carry together."

"And, how does that make you feel?"

Mike sat up straighter in his chair as he said, "Not as alone. It feels really good."

"I'd like to make an observation, Mike. As you said that, you smiled, sat more upright and looked right at me."

"That's funny, because I actually feel like I lost about twenty pounds, not from my waist but from my shoulders."

"What will that enable you to do?"

"It gives me more energy and more time. And, a few available brain cells. I think I'll be able to take on more CEO type tasks."

"And, what do you have to give up to keep this?"

"I have to avoid going backwards and not let the team delegate to me. I have to teach them some new skills, which means investing more time in the short term. The scary part is that I'll have to give up some control. Even though I was getting totally exhausted doing all the little things at least I knew they were getting done right. I will have to trust that the team will take on the responsibilities and follow through. Yeah, giving up control will probably be the hardest."

"What can you do to make it easier to give up control?"

"I have to give up the right duties and authority to the right person with the right training with the right controls and with the right measurements. That will give the team and me the best chance of success."

"Right!" Sandy laughed and said, "Sorry, I couldn't help but tease you a bit. What else did you learn?"

"I showed you the gaps and overlaps list that we made. I think that the overlaps relate to what we have just discussed, spreading the responsibility and authority in the company. If I think about the gaps, maybe they're also related to control and spreading the responsibility and authority."

"Interesting. Tell me more."

"I'm muddling through this right now but let me try out this idea. The gaps indicate that the members of the team were self-focused and did not focus on other team members, the customers or the suppliers. Is it possible that they didn't share information with each other either? Were they in a company culture that supported, maybe even encouraged, isolationism?"

"What does that mean?"

"I think that I need to create a movement across the organization, a real change in the culture. Now, that's a big job!"

Chapter 7: R = Reflect

It was quiet. Sandy was using another one of her long silences to give Mike a chance to digest what he had just said. Finally, she broke the silence.

"Mike, did you notice that I put your lists of gaps and overlaps on the floor?"

"I did. Wasn't sure what to make of it."

"It was not meant to be disrespectful of the work that you and your team did. You made amazing progress and the results show great insight about the current status of the company. It was meant to put the details out of your line of sight, so you could be above the details, literally, and think more broadly of the conclusions. You did just that. Now, I'm going to ask you to take another step and let go of the details and your conclusions. You have been living and breathing this company for eight weeks now with not a single break to reflect."

Sandy pulled out the laminated L.E.A.R.N.E.D Leader card and pointed to the "R".

"Reflect. You need some time to reflect, get perspective about the current situation and allow your creative brain cells to kick in."

"You are so right. I've been running at a thousand miles an hour and my brain cells are banging against each other. How do I get them re-aligned?"

"Lots of studies have shown that we have to step away from our problems in order to see the big picture and to see the path forward. You've done a great job in describing the situation in the company. Your lists of issues, opportunities, gaps and overlaps summarize the current state of the company. You now need to take the time to reflect on the situation and on yourself so you can visualize the future state of the company and how you will get there."

"What do you recommend?"

"Tell me about a place and time when you felt completely relaxed and open."

"That's easy. Marie's brother, Tom, has a vacation house on a lake in the Pocono Mountains, about two hours north of here. Three years ago, Marie and I went there for a long weekend. We spent hours sitting by the lake, walking in the woods, cooking and talking. I read an entire novel in just two days. It was such a short time but we really felt rejuvenated by the break. Tom has been telling us to use the cabin whenever we want, but we have been too busy to do it. I'm sure if I called him, he would be thrilled to let us have a weekend vacation. "

"Sounds perfect. So I suggest that you and Marie relax for the weekend and don't think about work at all. Leave all of your work stuff at home. No laptop. Let the staff know that you should be contacted for emergencies only. Take a book you'd like to read. And, take a new, small notebook so you can record your thoughts. Let the dust settle and come back with your brain cells re-aligned."

Reflections at the Lake

Marie was overjoyed when Mike suggested a weekend at Tom's house on the lake. With the warm weather that felt more like mid-June than mid-May, the flowers were in full bloom. If the water wasn't freezing cold, they might even take the kayaks out for a leisurely trip across the lake. It was just what they needed to reconnect and relax. Although it was only a two hour drive, they arrived after dark on Friday and fell, exhausted, into the king sized bed.

Saturday morning arrived bright and sunny. Marie was up early, enjoying watching the birds and squirrels hop from tree to tree. She was completely relaxed. Mike was sound asleep and she debated with herself about waking him so he could enjoy the view or letting him get the much needed sleep. When 10:00 arrived, she brewed another pot of coffee and started cooking a thick slab of bacon. The smell would wake Mike.

"Could life be any better than this?" said Mike as he hugged Marie. "Coffee, bacon, eggs, and the most beautiful view in the world, my wonderful wife. And, the view out the window is not that bad either."

Marie laughed. Mike already seemed more relaxed than she had seen him in weeks. As the food disappeared they planned their weekend. They would spend the rest of Saturday on the lake and on the trails, Saturday evening dinner at a country inn about ten minutes away, another big breakfast Sunday morning, checking out antique shops in the afternoon and a slow drive home, stopping at any cute store that caught their eyes.

Saturday afternoon the sun glinted off the water of Arrowhead Lake. Mike and Marie had walked almost three quarters of the perimeter when they got to the swimming area. The sandy beach was deserted now but in a few weeks lots of noisy, water splashing, over-active kids would take over this area. They strolled past the playground with its variety of swings, seesaws, slides and climbing equipment. At least ten children were in the playground but six of them were clinging to an old, wooden merry-go-round structure and laughing loudly. The cone-shaped unit clanged against the center pole, like a giant bell. The children were shifting positions around the perimeter to try to balance the triangular cone so that it would spin freely.

"Now, that's a throw-back to my childhood," said Mike. "That was called a witch's hat in my neighborhood. If you shifted the kids around the edge until the weight was balanced then it would spin really fast. Of course, that was until one of the kids let go and was hurled across the gravel. Fewer lawyers back then. Boy it was fun. I thought they had been outlawed years ago."

"It does look dangerous…but fun," added Marie as they sat down on a bench to watch. "I hope there's no blood."

They watched the children maneuver around the edge of the witch's hat, until it was eventually balanced. It began to spin smoothly and was really picking up speed. The laughs and screams got louder as the children leaned back to get the most momentum.

Mike took his little notebook from his pocket and sketched a drawing of the witch's hat.

"Marie, I know that we had agreed not to talk business this weekend, but Sandy told me to bring along this little notebook to jot down my reflections. I think she meant for me to really step away from the day-to-day business and reflect on the big picture. Look at the kids on that merry-go-round. They struggled to find the right positions on the three sides. They collaborated to get the balance just right. And, when everything was in balance, it seemed to take off as if there was a huge motor spinning it."

"Right, did you see the really tall kid move back and forth to counterbalance the two smaller kids on the other side?"

"Balance. Marie, I think that's what's missing at Square One. Balance."

Marie shifted on the bench to look at Mike. "What do you mean?"

"Let me show you."

Mike handed Marie his notebook and showed her a sketch he had just finished.

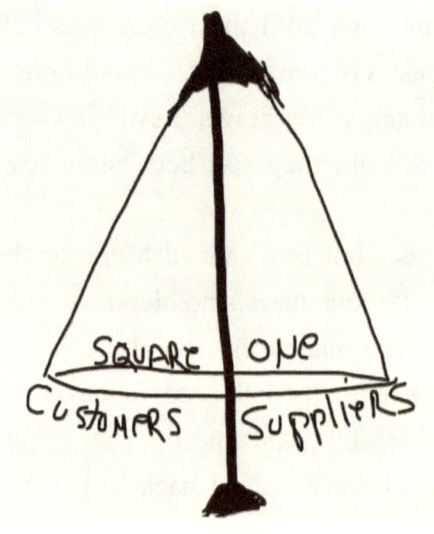

"I think Square One has put all of its attention on its own operation and not much attention on the customers and suppliers. All of our weight is on that side of the circle. We are out of balance. We haven't been spinning. We are bumping into the pole!"

"You were telling me that in your planning sessions you identified that one of the gaps related to understanding the needs of the customers and the capabilities of suppliers. It's an interesting way of illustrating it."

"Let me take it one step more. Maybe it's more like this."

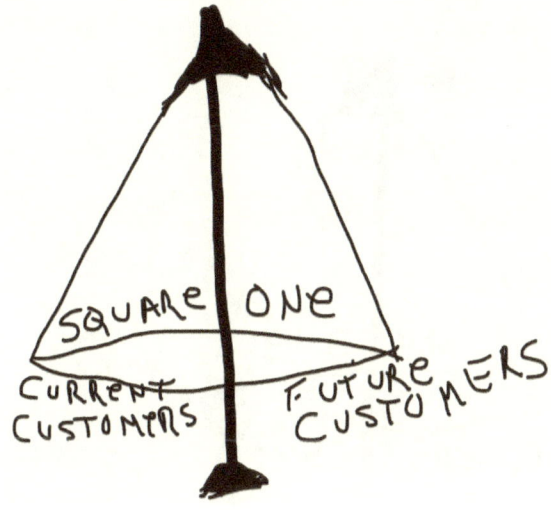

"We are out of balance with our current customers and our future customers. We didn't know until it was too late that one of our customers may no longer need our product in their process. I'm afraid that some of our team has been so focused on future projects that we are ignoring our current customers and any future needs they may have. If our current customers jump off the merry-go-round we'll be even more out of balance."

"And, yes, we seem to have the same problem when we look at our overall supply chain. We haven't taken advantage of building relationships with our suppliers. And, boy, part of that is my fault. When I was a consultant, I just did the projects that Don

95

asked us to do. I didn't know the big picture or how the supply chain fit into the whole operation. We've been surprised by changes some of the suppliers made and it hurt our customers. And, I think some of the team is not even sure who our competitors are. We've really lost sight of them. Again, out of balance. Definitely not spinning!"

Mike continued to draw and showed Marie another picture.

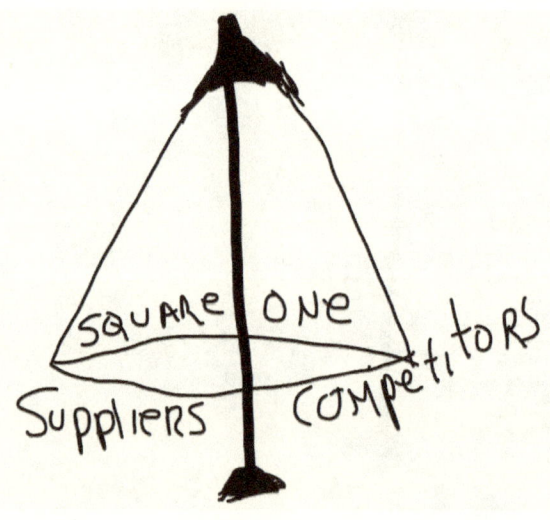

"Now when I think about the overlaps that we identified, I think we are out of balance there too. We have not been balancing authority with responsibility. That's why I have been spending so much of my time on the detailed work in the business. But I think there is another component here as well, capability. If someone has the responsibility and authority to carry out tasks but they are not fully trained or capable, it'll be a disaster. On the other hand, I think some members of the team are very well qualified and have not been challenged with enough responsibilities and authority. These team members are bored and we may be at risk of losing some of our best talent."

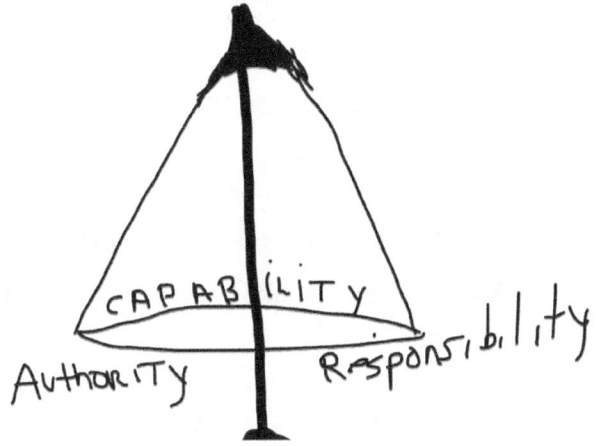

"The other overlap was in the organizational systems. We need to balance increased efficiency while maintaining quality and internal control."

"We need to get things done right, efficiently, but also to maintain checks and balances that keep an organization strong and on the right side of the laws and regulations."

Mike paused and studied his sketches for a moment while watching the kids on the witch's hat. Suddenly one of the kids

97

yelled "off" and jumped off the unit. It crashed into the pole and swung wildly. It quickly stopped spinning. The kids started to signal and shift and the tall kid shouted directions to the others. "Jeff move to where Billy was." "Kathy move closer to Jeff." The rest of the kids shifted around the perimeter until it was again rebalanced and started to spin freely.

"Did you see that, Marie?" Mike asked. "Did you see how quickly they readjusted their positions? Agility. Flexibility in roles. Teamwork. A leader giving direction. Keeping your eye on the goal of spinning freely."

Mike quickly sketched another witch's hat with the words Leadership, Agility and Teamwork around the base.

"I think this is an important one for my team," said Mike. "I need to not only be the leader, but to develop leadership in my team. They need to be agile, flexible and open minded about finding new solutions for the company and we all need to work as a team. I think this hat is my favorite so far."

"Mike, I like the visual you're using. It makes it easy for me to see the issues. I think your team will relate to these images. Can I add one more drawing for you to consider?"

Marie took the notebook and after a minute handed it back to Mike with her drawing.

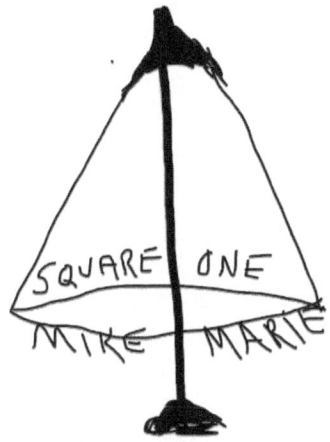

"I want this to remind you that you and I need to also balance our lives with the company as well as with each other."

Mike pulled Marie towards him and gave her a long hug.

"I will never forget that you and I are in this together, Marie. I couldn't do it alone and I wouldn't want to. I was wrong. This is my favorite hat."

"We better stop smooching in front of all those kids," said Marie with a huge smile on her face. "The other thing I learned today is that it's a good thing neither of us wanted to be an artist!"

Mike tucked his notebook into his pocket again. He had a satisfied grin on his face.

"Thanks for letting me ramble on...or should I say 'reflect'. I'm feeling so much better about wrapping my hands around the issues at work. But, what's really strange is that I feel that I also have a better handle on the question of whether or not I'm the right guy for the job. I feel a weight lifting from my shoulders. How about if we continue our vacation? We still have a long way to finish our walk around the lake. Can we fit in a short nap before dinner?"

Balance

When Sandy walked into Mike's office on Tuesday morning, she saw a big difference in him. He was smiling and sitting very upright in his chair. He emanated an energy that she had not seen in him in the past. Then she noticed a strange "sculpture" on his desk.

"Looks like the weekend of reflection did you a world of good, Mike. You look great."

"Thanks, Sandy. I feel great. You know that I was reluctant to go away for two whole days but, wow, did it make a difference. I really get what you said about letting go of the details and opening up my mind to new directions. Marie and I enjoyed every minute. We ate well, walked, enjoyed nature, talked and reconnected. My scale said that I gained two pounds but the weight that lifted from my shoulders was about fifty pounds so I really came out ahead!"

"And, what's this?" Sandy said as she pointed to the sculpture.

"That was my 'ah-ha' moment, my witch's hat" said Mike as he proudly pointed to the odd object on his desk. He lifted it up to reveal a three inch round base made of modeling clay and a seven inch long stick with a rounded top stuck in the middle of the base. Perched on top of the stick was a three sided funnel that swiveled freely. Attached to each side was a sticky note.

Mike told Sandy about sitting at the playground and watching the kids on the witch's hat. He described how they maneuvered around the perimeter until it was balanced and how fast it spun when they achieved the right balance of weight. He told her of the one kid who jumped off and how the rest quickly responded by rebalancing their weight. Mike brought out his notebook and showed Sandy the sketches. He described the ways he thought that the company was out of balance and how balance would allow the company to move as fast as the witch's hat. He used the sticky notes with words that represented the key relationships to illustrate where they needed to rebalance.

"I'm impressed, Mike. I love having the visual to illustrate the concepts. What will you do to share this with your team?"

"Last night I found this three-sided funnel at the auto store. I bought enough so I can give each person on the team their own witch's hat at our team meeting tomorrow morning. I'm going to ask them to use different size and colors of sticky notes to show three areas that need to be in balance. I'll ask them to think about balance within their own areas and also between their teams and other teams as well as outside groups. I'm going to ask them to think about how to achieve balance but then how to be agile to rebalance when needed."

"Sounds like a great way to open the discussion and follow up on your gaps and overlaps. What's the next step?"

Mike looked at Sandy quizzically. "Not sure what you're asking. I think this model will let us explore our problems."

"I agree. At the end of the meeting you'll have a detailed picture of 'what is'. By that I mean what is the current situation in the company. Great. You get it. They get it. So what?"

"I don't know. I was so excited that I finally understood the big picture of what was going on, I stopped at that. I guess you're telling me I'm just at the starting block."

The Trusted Team

"Mike, I love that while you were relaxing over the weekend, you had the experience of seeing something with new eyes. I would ask you to think about the kids again. It sounds like the kids were working as a team with one of them acting as the team leader."

"True. They signaled each other about positions on the perimeter. And, just before the kid jumped off, he yelled that he was jumping. The other kids were able to brace themselves for when the witch's hat hit the pole and then to organize their shifting of positions. It seemed so smooth."

"What allowed the kids to work together so well?"

"Obviously, they had done this before. They knew how to make it spin. But they also seemed to care about each other. If the kid had not let them know he was jumping off the rest of them could have been surprised and maybe fallen off and been hurt. They worked together to make it spin really fast."

"So, how would you sum it up?"

"I think they trusted each other. Yeah, I guess it was trust."

"If they didn't trust each other, would they get the witch's hat to spin?"

"I don't think so. They would be worried and maybe scared. They wouldn't know if everybody wanted to help or if somebody would drag their feet... literally. They wouldn't know who to listen to. It could be chaos. It certainly would not have been fun."

"Mike, early in our coaching sessions you told me about how the team called you 'Boss' instead of using your name. You thought that maybe it was a signal that they didn't trust you. Can I ask you to reflect on that and on trust in your team?"

"I remember that conversation very well. It was one of my first 'ah-ha' moments. And my suspicions seemed to be verified. At that time they did not trust me. At all. But, I think that over the past several weeks, I've been making some headway."

"What makes you think that they're developing trust?"

"I think the team meetings have helped. They are speaking up. Last week one of the team members openly discussed something that wasn't going so well and asked the others for suggestions. I try to be open about the positives and the negatives. I think they are beginning to see that I can do the job. But I have also let them see that I don't know everything. I ask for help when I need it."

"So what do you think may still be missing?"

"I don't know. I need to think about that."

"May I tell you about my experiences in building trust in a team?"

"I'm all ears!"

"I have found trust is a rather squishy thing. Sometimes it's hard to define but we know it when we see it …or feel it. I define trust as the gift we share with someone who is trustworthy. To have trust in an organization, the team members must act in a trustworthy manner, just like the kids on the witch's hat in the playground. I break down trustworthiness into five components. When I think of these elements of trustworthiness, it's easier to figure out where we're making progress and where we need to rebuild."

"That makes sense but I've never heard trustworthiness broken down into parts. What are the five components of trustworthiness?"

Sandy got up and wrote on the whiteboard.

> **Components of Trustworthiness**
> 1. **Competence – ability**
> 2. **Integrity – doing the right thing**
> 3. **Openness – authenticity**
> 4. **Benevolence – having the best interests of others in mind**
> 5. **Shared vision – individual vision and organizational visions are congruent**

"Let me give you some examples," said Sandy. "If your church was interviewing for a new minister, how would these elements of trustworthiness affect your selection process?"

"That's easy. He would have to know the church rules, the religious doctrine and be competent in running a church. He would have to have a pure heart and always do the right thing so he could set an example for the rest of us. I would want him to be open and to accept everyone as equal members of the church and let us get to know him as well. Of course he would have to have the best interests of the congregation in mind as he made decisions. I wouldn't want him to be thinking of himself first. And he would have to share the congregation's vision of the role the church would play in everyone's life. I see how these components of trustworthiness would help make that decision."

"Now, a bit tougher question, if you're looking for a tax accountant to do your taxes, who do you select?"

"He would have to know the tax law, for sure. And, I'd want him to be honest. I see. In that case competence and integrity are really important."

"Right. Are the rest important?"

"As I think about it, yes, they are. I'd want him to be open about what he knows and if there are areas of the tax rules that are not his area of expertise. And, I do want him to have my best interests in mind. I'd want him to get the job done and meet the deadlines. I'd want to stay on the right side of the law but not overpay in taxes. I'd want him to go the extra mile to be sure that I get the best advice. Shared vision could mean that he has to understand that I want to stay out of jail and don't want to break any of the rules and he has to believe in that approach as well."

"Now think about an organization. Suppose you are interviewing for a job in a new company, how could this approach help you decide if the organization was trustworthy?"

"Interesting. I don't think I ever thought of an organization as trustworthy or not trustworthy but these components of trustworthiness seem to fit organizations as well. A competent organization would have a strong place in its market. Customers would respect the organization and the products or services. Employees would see management and co-workers as credible. Integrity in an organization is really important. The management, the employees and the policies have to be ethical even when it's not easy. An organization with openness would not just accept diversity, but embrace it. The organization would be tolerant of new ideas and allow people to try new things, which also means allowing them to fail sometimes. A benevolent organization would have policies that are fair and supportive of management and of the employees but also for suppliers and customers. Shared vision is something that I've seen as a gap in many organizations. The guy at the top knows where the company is headed but he keeps it a secret. I can see how all of these components are important in an organization."

"What would it look like and feel like to work in a company that was strong in all of the components of trustworthiness?"

"No politics, low bureaucracy, fast decision-making, mutual respect, universal fairness, great customer relations, employee loyalty, confidence in the future at all levels, well-trained employees, creative people, caring for each other, overall well-being. I could go on and on but in a single word, awesome."

"The components of trustworthiness allow us to decide if a person, a team or an organization should receive the gift of our trust."

"It makes sense. So if I think of the kids, they were competent because they understood the concept of balancing their weights and they sure knew how to get that witch's hat spinning fast. They had integrity and treated each other as friends and with respect. No bullying. I don't know if they have 'openness' except that nobody got mad at the kid who jumped off and there were both girls and boys of all sizes and shapes playing together. They all seemed to have the best interests of the group in mind because they collaborated, suggesting how to rebalance and taking the directions of the leader. And vision. I think the vision was to go fast and they worked toward that together."

"I agree. They demonstrated the components of trustworthiness and it resulted in a trusting team. Now, what about your team? You mentioned some things that seem to be working. How does that fit into the components of trustworthiness?"

"I'm letting them see that I am competent and I'm telling them when I see them acting in a competent way. I think most of the team members are very competent, but there are a few issues. Integrity is one of my core values. I think I demonstrate that in the way I'm making decisions. But I probably should discuss my core values and talk about them more openly, not expect them to pick up my intent but to insist that the entire team acts with integrity. I need to discuss it more. Openness is hard for me. I try to be authentic but it's hard for me to let them get to know me. This is another one I need to work on. Benevolence. They know that Don was like a father to me. And that I am trying to build on his legacy. I think that I'm showing that I have the best interests of the team in mind. Shared vision is another weak point. I definitely need to spend some time on that one."

"Mike, may I make an observation?"

"Of course."

"During this session you talked about the need to gain balance and agility. You observed that in order to do this, you need a team that is trustworthy and trusts each other."

"You captured the last hour into one sentence!"

"Can I ask you to formulate a direction from this work? Write it on the board."

Mike stood up and wrote on the whiteboard.

I want to have a trusted team to achieve balance and agility in order to move the company forward.

Chapter 8: N = Navigate the Way Forward

Sandy pulled out her laminated card again and motioned for Mike to do the same.

"N is for navigate the way forward. So for the moment, think of Square One as a ship in the ocean that got tossed about during a huge storm. You just figured out where you are. You now know the longitude and the latitude and from that you can find out the currents and tides. Now what?"

"I have to get the ship going forward again."

"Where is forward?"

"…the right direction?"

"OK, what direction is the right direction?"

"That depends."

"Depends on what?"

"Depends on where home port is, I guess. Or, wherever the ship was heading before the storm."

"Ah, so you need to determine where the ship is heading before you determine if it's going in the right direction. Is that what you said?"

"Right. We need a destination."

"What else do you need?"

"A roadmap? A set of directions?"

"So, I think I hear you say that to navigate the ship you need to know the destination and you need a map of routes to get there. Did I get that right?"

"Duh, now that you summarized it, it sounds pretty obvious. But I was about to jump into action and just go somewhere. It seemed better than doing nothing. But I see what you're saying. If I just move the company in a direction, then I may be moving it closer to our ultimate goal or maybe moving it farther away. I need to look at various ways of getting there and select the route that looks most promising. I think I see what you mean. We have to figure out what 'new and improved' looks like, where to go from here and how do we get there. So, what's the next step?"

Determining the Destination – Where do we want to be?

Mike's session with Sandy was exhilarating. Again, he was amazed at how his time with his coach clarified his thinking. He felt that she continued to gently guide him but never told him what to do.

Mike leaned back in his chair and re-read the words he had written on the whiteboard.

> **I want to have a trusted team to achieve balance and agility in order to move the company forward.**

"I guess the next challenge is to change the word 'forward' to a specific and achievable goal," Mike said to himself. "This is not something I should do alone…or in my office…or in isolation. This is the vision that we need to create. Shared vision. That's one of Sandy's elements of a trustworthy organization. I guess if we create the vision together then working together to reach it will be easier. I think the first step is to decide who should be involved in the planning phase. I can't get consensus from everyone in the company. But there are key people who must be involved. Of course, Anne is critical in this effort. And, the rest of the board…probably."

Mike pulled out a tablet and created a table with headings across the top:

- Name
- Why should he/she be involved?
- What will he/she contribute?

He began to fill in the table and came up with a list of over twenty people, all with something to contribute to the effort and a good reason to be involved.

"Too many" Mike said. "Not a good working group."

Mike went back to his table and added one more heading

- Role in the Process

He decided to define the roles as 1) defining the vision and mission for the entire company; 2) Converting the mission into strategic goals; and, 3) Converting goals into action plans. As he filled in the final column he realized that some people spanned two roles and others would be best in a single role.

"Step one" said Mike. "Define the vision and mission".

Mike picked up his phone and called Anne to schedule a meeting with her.

Vision and Mission Clarified

Although Mike had weekly phone calls with Anne and monthly meetings with the Board to keep them informed and to get their input on operations, this meeting would be different. In the past, the mission and vision of the company reflected Don's thinking. Don was solely responsible for developing the direction for the company and getting everyone to jump on his bandwagon. Mike knew that Don's approach wouldn't work now. The mission and vision would have to be co-created by the Board with his input.

"Good morning, everyone," said Mike as he stood to get the attention of the seven board members. "I'd like to call this meeting to order. Thank you for coming and for setting aside additional time today to accomplish what I think is a critical step for the future of the company. We need to answer the question 'what do we want Square One to look like in five years?'."

For the next four hours Mike facilitated a lively discussion of core values, strategic goals, operational goals, financial goals, market positioning and new product development. They outlined the strengths, weaknesses, threats and opportunities for the company. They reviewed the history of the company, Don's vision and where the company was now. They talked about industry trends, changes in business climate and innovations in the field. By five o'clock the waste can was overflowing with stained coffee cups, the whiteboards were covered with flow charts and the rest of the walls were decorated with flip chart paper. It looked like a successful meeting.

Mike finally sat down. He didn't realize how much his feet hurt. His face beamed as he looked around the room. The Board members looked almost as exhausted as he did. "Thank you. I think we accomplished a lot today."

Mike had typed the product of the afternoon's work into his computer and printed a copy for each Board member.

Square One, Inc.

Vision Statement

The Vision of Square One is to be the "go to" source for outstanding quality specialty chemicals and formulations.

Mission Statement

The Mission of Square One is to build a financially fit and growing company that teams with our customers, suppliers and employees to identify emerging needs and meet current needs with a full complement of the highest quality specialty chemicals and formulations on the market at a competitive price, with timely delivery and always acting with honesty and integrity.

"Thank you, Mike. I think you captured our efforts into a very succinct and inspiring vision and mission for the company," said Anne. "If we can achieve this, then I, personally, will feel that we are successful. I think Don would not only agree, but he would be applauding you right now."

As the other board members' heads nodded in agreement, Anne said "I move that we accept the Vision and Mission Statements as presented." Anne's motion was followed by a quick second and a round of "yes" votes. Unanimous!

"Again, thank you for your time and your support in this effort," said Mike. "Next step will be developing the Goals for the next five years in order to achieve this Mission. I will circle back to present those goals and get your approval before we proceed to an action plan."

"I move to adjourn this very successful meeting" said Anne.

Dinner and Marie's Perspective

Mike was exhausted by the intensity of the afternoon but excited to tell Marie about the progress. He walked in the door with the Vision and Mission Statement in his hand. Marie turned from the stove, spatula in hand and offered Mike a taste of the Korean-style pulled pork that was warming on the stove.

"You look …different," said Marie. "I was going to say tired but that wasn't right. Then I thought hyper but maybe that's too much. Ok, spill it. How did the big meeting go?"

"Great. All I can say is, Great! And, this pork is also great!" Mike laughed and handed Marie the piece of paper.

"Wow," said Marie. "I like it…a lot. I can picture this hanging on the wall. Employees and visitors would appreciate it."

"Marie, you know that I have been overwhelmed by taking on this role. I doubted that I was the right person to run the company. But, today, I felt right at home. I loved leading the Board to a defined direction. I'm excited about taking this to the employees. After our weekend away I became much more comfortable that I understand where the company is, its strengths and weaknesses. When I shared my witch's hat drawings with Sandy in our last meeting she was really encouraging and I felt that I was on a good path. Sandy said that the next step to becoming a L.E.A.R.N.E.D. Leader was the "N" to navigate the way forward. She said that we needed a destination and a roadmap. This Vision and Mission Statement is the destination. When I take this to the management team and we agree on strategic goals and an action plan, we will have the roadmap. So, to answer your question about how I feel…yes, tired, yes, hyped…and oh so good! Let's eat, I also feel starved."

Step Two – The Goals

Monday morning Mike had the conference room set up for the Goal Setting meeting. Eric, Sally, Jessica, John, Todd, Alan and Jennifer filed in and took their usual seats. They were somewhat surprised to find Anne joining them for the meeting. At each seat was an agenda and a copy of the new Vision and Mission Statement. Mike also had the Vision and Mission Statements projected on the wall.

Anne opened the meeting by summarizing the discussion that had occurred at the board meeting, slowly reading the Vision and Mission Statements then opening the floor for questions. A few clarifying questions were asked but in general, the management team nodded and listened intently.

Mike followed by summarizing his conversation with his coach, Sandy, and explaining that having a destination and a roadmap was critical to the success of the business. The Vision and Mission Statement was the destination. Their task was to translate the Mission into a series of achievable and measurable goals. More nods and smiles.

"I suggest that we take apart the Vision and Mission Statements into little chunks and describe goals that help us to get to those parts. Let's start with the first phrase 'to be a fit and growing company'."

Mike turned to Eric and said, "How would you define fit and growing?"

Eric looked around the room with a thoughtful glance. "I think fit would be financially sound, so that our profitability is stable and, maybe even growing. I think it also means that we have enough cash on hand or accessible to fund the projects that we want to do in order to grow. And, that we have procedures and policies in place that give us confidence in our numbers. Growing is another question. We can think of it as growing in revenue or growing in profitability or both. The easy part is that we can set numerical goals for these and track our progress."

"Jen, what about 'outstanding quality'?" Mike asked.

"Again, pretty easy. If we know the quality standards that our customers want and need, we can set a goal of meeting those standards one hundred percent of the time. I know I'm jumping ahead, but that includes competitive price and timely delivery in the definition of quality."

Mike highlighted the words 'specialty chemicals and formulations' on the projected copy of the Vision. "Let's talk about what this includes and, more important, what it excludes."

"Right," said Todd. "I like that it excludes commodity or large volume chemicals. Our operations are just not set up for large scale production."

"And," added John, "that's a different customer group. We are not known in that market and would have a hard time competing with the big boys. But what does that mean for our base products? They are somewhat like commodity products. Does that mean we stop making and selling them?"

Jessica's hand popped up to get attention. "I think we need to consider the words 'full complement and 'meeting needs' when we decide about our base products. If we can provide products to meet all of the customers' needs because we also provide the base products then I think it meets the mission."

Mike encouraged the dialog on this topic until the consensus was that the team needed more information about how the customers were using the base products in order to decide how they fit with the new mission.

"Now let's look at the words 'team with customers, suppliers and employees' and think about what that means," said Mike.

Jessica and Todd glanced at each other and smiled. Todd spoke first. "Mike, Jess and I have been talking about the gap that we identified in our meeting, that we don't understand the wants and needs of our current and future customers. We think it's critical that we address this immediately. I am really glad that the Board recognizes this as a priority and put it in our Mission."

Jessica nodded and added "The other gap was that we aren't finding ways to optimize opportunities with competitors and suppliers. This part of the mission covers that goal as well. I think it's really cool that the management team and the Board arrived at similar conclusions but came at it from different directions. It makes me feel comfortable that the Board will support our efforts in this area."

Eric nodded at Jessica and Todd. "As long as you brought up our gaps, I'd like to remind everyone of our overlaps as well. We said that we should align authority so it matches responsibility and to redesign systems to maximize efficiency without giving up quality and internal control mechanisms. I really support working on those goals and I think that they mirror this Mission Statement as well. I'm not sure if this says that *we* are really smart or if the Board is really smart."

Eric's last comment got the intended laugh, especially from Anne.

Sally looked at Mike and Anne. "Thank you for emphasizing the words "honesty and integrity" in the Mission Statement. These core values were really important to Don and I feel very strongly that we were successful in the past because of his commitment to staying true to his core values."

"You are so right, Sally," said Anne. "Don was a man of true integrity. That legacy will always be critical to all of us."

By the end of the four hour meeting, the team had a detailed list of goals with measurable outcomes, timeframes and accountabilities.

"Thank you," said Mike. "This team has done a great job."

Anne stood and held up her almost-empty coffee cup in a toast. "To us and a great future together."

Chapter 9: E = Engage all Stakeholders

Mike was anxious to tell Sandy about his progress in defining the destination and the roadmap. He printed the Vision and Mission Statements and the list of goals that the management team had described. Each goal followed the SMART rule. It was Specific, Measurable, Achievable, had a Responsible person assigned and had a Timeframe.

When Sandy finished reading the documents, she handed them back to Mike. "Great work, Mike. You have a destination and a roadmap. I think 'N' is done. Time to move on to the 'E' in the L.E.A.R.N.E.D. Leader."

"Right. E is for Engage. I think I may have already done that as well. The Board was fully engaged in writing the Vision and Mission. Then Anne also worked on the Goal Setting Committee. She took our goals back to the Board and they enthusiastically endorsed them. So, can I skip that letter?"

"I think you did a big part of the 'E', Mike, but not all. Who else needs to be on board for this plan to be successful? Who else will be involved in the implementation?"

"Oh, implementation....I guess the rest of the staff, the employees...?"

"Yes. Remember when we talked about trust and that shared vision is a key part of building trust in an organization? What can you do to share this vision with the rest of the staff? What can you do to engage them in the success of this effort?"

"I see your point, Sandy. I was thinking of engaging only in the direction of management and the Board, upward engagement, but I need to engage the rest of the employees. Actually, it's the staff that will make this successful, not the Board, so I missed the most important part of the 'E', didn't I?"

"Not uncommon. We tend to think of 'selling' our ideas up the organization, not down into the ranks. What will make the rest of the staff buy into this plan?"

"I think they need to understand it, so first I should meet with small groups to tell them about the process that we have used so far. They need to feel that their work is critical to our future. They need to hear me commit to the plan and our future together. I think that I should also find some measurements that we can use to monitor our overall progress and keep them informed."

"What will those measurements look like?"

"Sandy, I think one of my greatest frustrations in the past was when management would talk about changes in share price, or revenue or profits. I couldn't affect those measurements so it made me feel helpless. I think that we need to develop measurements for each department and each group that relate to what the individuals do so that they see the impact of their work."

"I couldn't agree with you more, Mike. The staff needs to feel not only engaged but that their work has an impact. I appreciate that you recognize this and will make it a priority. May I also suggest that you tell the staff what you are trying to do and get some input?"

"I will, Sandy. Thanks. Those discussions will definitely help me to achieve the 'E'.

"These are great ideas, Mike. Who on the management team can help in this part of the project?"

"Again, your questions make me realize that I'm missing a huge chunk of important steps. It can't be just me. The employees have to see and hear this commitment from everyone on the management team. I'll make sure that my team gives a consistent message. What about Anne? Should I bring her into some of the employee meetings?"

"Interesting question. Can I take off my coach hat and give you my opinion?"

"Of course."

"Asking Anne to attend all of the employee meetings may be a drain on her time. But if she attends only some of the meetings, the employees may read more into that than you want. So, I suggest that you have an all-company meeting with Anne and maybe a few other Board members. They can set the tone and clearly express their commitment to the program. Everyone will hear the same thing."

"I like that. I'm sure that at least two other Board members will make the time to come to a meeting. Maybe, we should make it a really festive occasion. Very upbeat."

"Great. That will show the employees that you and the Board are positive and confident."

"I think you already know that I am a very visual thinker. I would like to find some small symbol of the new direction and present it at that meeting. Tee shirts, mugs, something nice that they will use and value."

"I also love symbols because they constantly remind us of what's important. I like the idea and really support that the item is special or novel, not just another throw away item."

Sandy sat back and let a gentle silence fall. Then she said, "Let's round out the 'E', Mike. What other groups need to be engaged in order for this to work?"

The puzzled look on Mike's face made Sandy giggle. "Stumped?" she said, but let the silence continue.

Mike knew better than to just fill the silence with chatter. After about five minutes, his face brightened. "Of course," he said, "the suppliers and customers."

"Right. Your management team felt very strongly that the balance between Square One, the suppliers and the customers needed to be re-adjusted. This a great opportunity to do that and to have them support you in this new strategic direction. What approach could you take?"

"Again, not something I would attempt alone. I think I'll set up two cross-functional teams, one to work with the suppliers and one to work with the customers, so we can show them that we're bringing lots of resources to this."

Sandy let out a huge sigh. "I now pronounce 'E' complete!"

All Aboard!

The Ship Inn Restaurant had just the right atmosphere and décor for the Square One Company meeting. Mike and the management team decided to invite all of the employees to bring their spouses or significant others. They knew that to make this strategic plan achievable, everyone in the company would have to put in a hundred and ten percent. They also knew that many employees were trying to reassure their families that Don's passing would not cause the company to fail. Mike was pleasantly surprised when all of the Board members were enthusiastic about coming and were also bringing their spouses.

The evening was pleasantly warm and the atmosphere in the room was electric. At each seat was a name card and an agenda. At the side of the room was a long table with beautifully wrapped boxes, each with the name of an employee or a Board Member. The candles flickered and the jazz trio played softly in the background. Everyone was dressed for the occasion and there was good natured joking about not recognizing each other in their "Sunday" clothes. After the cocktail hour the program began when Mike walked to the podium.

"Thank you all for coming and making this a special night. Of course, Anne needs no introduction, but I'm going to introduce her anyway. I knew Anne and Don for over ten years. Don was like a father to me. I know that Don would agree with me when I say that without Anne's strength and guidance, Square One would not be here. With her continuing support, we will all take Square One to a new destination. Please welcome Anne Smith."

Anne walked to the podium and hugged Mike.

"Dear friends. I also thank you for making this a special night. It has been five months since we lost Don. I lost my best friend and life partner. It has been a hard time for me personally. But what I have realized, more than ever, is that I am surrounded by best friends....all of you."

Anne took a brief moment to let her words be heard and to compose herself. She clicked on the projector and the image of a beautiful water-color painting of a six mast sailing ship came up on the screen. At the same time, she pulled a black velvet cover off of the original painting. The audience let out an appreciative sigh. The name painted on the hull of the ship was Square One.

"This painting will hang in the lobby of Square One to remind us of the journey that we are about to embark upon. With the Board, Mike, the management team and all of you, we will sail our ship to a bright future. Welcome aboard!"

It took almost ten minutes for the applause to die down. The nods, back slapping and hand shaking across tables continued for another five minutes. Finally, Anne rapped on the podium.

"I would like to summarize for all of you the process that we used to find our destination and to set the course to get there."

The absolute silence was a complete contrast to the earlier pandemonium. The audience listened attentively as Anne spent the next twenty minutes describing the strategic plan. When Anne was finished she introduced each of the Board members and thanked them for their service.

"And, finally, I must recognize Mike." Anne turned to Mike so that although she spoke into the microphone, it felt like a personal conversation.

"Mike, you were thrown into a big job without warning. I can never thank you enough for jumping in with both feet. I know that this has taken a toll on you and also on Marie. We owe you

....big time!" Applause and a standing ovation followed Anne's comments to Mike.

"And, now, please go to the side table and get the box with your name on it." After waiting until everyone was reseated, Anne said, "Now, open the boxes, please. There was an excited rustling of paper and hundreds of ohs and ahs. Each employee and Board member had received a signed limited edition print of the original painting, in a gold leaf frame.

With an ear-to-ear grin, Anne said "All Aboard! Let's enjoy this journey together!"

Chapter 10: D = Do

"Mike, thank you for inviting me to the company dinner," said Sandy. "I was honored to be there. I can't remember a more moving and inspiring evening."

"Without you, Sandy, the evening probably would not have happened. Your coaching has been instrumental in helping me. I don't know where we would be without you."

"Thanks for the compliment, Mike. But I just asked the questions. You did the work. You carried the ball and made the touchdowns. You should be very proud of what you have accomplished in just over five months."

"Let's both pat ourselves on the back for just a few minutes."

"Deal."

Sandy sat back in her chair. Mike had been observing Sandy for long enough that he recognized that this body language meant that a challenging question was just about to come out of her mouth. And, he wasn't wrong.

"Mike, the past five and a half months have zoomed by. But there is one big question still sitting out there. Early in our coaching relationship, you said that you weren't sure if you were the right person for the job. Obviously, you have made a significant impact on the company so far. But to commit to continue as President and to eventually become the new owner is a big decision."

Again, Sandy pulled out her laminated card with The L.E.A.R.N.E.D. Leader acronym. "We have almost reached the end. D is for Do. Implementing the plan and achieving the goals you set for the company is a whole lot of 'do'. You have spent a lot of time ensuring that the management team and the employees know their roles and have set them on their journeys. Now you need to decide what part you want to play. What will you do?"

"You know that I have struggled with this. The journey so far has been exhilarating, fun, stressful and challenging. I must admit that it has taken a toll on Marie as well. Can I ask Marie to make this a permanent part of our lives? That's asking a lot. This has to be a joint decision."

"What will you do to finalize your decision?"

"I'm going to circle back to the 'R', if that's OK. I need to reflect. I think that I'll ask Marie to go back to the Poconos for the weekend. We could use the getaway and you are so right about taking the time to reflect to get a clear picture of what to do. I'll let you know my decision when we meet next week."

The Decision

August in the Pocono Mountains of Pennsylvania means warm, sparkling lakes, lush greenery, and lazy days. Marie was thrilled that Mike suggested the weekend getaway. Although Mike seemed to be enthusiastic about the new direction at Square One, the long hours and stress were obviously taking a toll on him. He missed dinner at least four nights a week, coming home well after 10:00 pm and falling into bed. His loosely hanging clothes were a constant reminder to Marie of the almost twenty pounds he had lost over the past five and a half months. Marie reveled in Mike's success at the dinner to launch the company's new strategic plan. She was bursting with pride when everyone in the room stood and the room shook with applause. But she was also afraid that they were drifting apart. She didn't want to be married to a successful and powerful man, she wanted to be married to *her* man.

Marie also knew that with Mike missing so many dinners together, he hadn't noticed that for the past six weeks she had given up wine. They had always talked about having children "some day" but "that day" arrived as a surprise. This weekend was the perfect time to break the news. Marie was not sure what Mike's reaction would be. She didn't know if he would share her happiness and excitement. But she did know that it would complicate his decision about whether or not to continue as President of Square One. And, she did know that if he really wanted to continue as President, adding a new baby into the mix would certainly complicate their lives.

Mike and Marie arrived at the cabin after 11:00 pm on Friday night and fell into bed. Saturday morning was bright and beautiful. They lounged in bed enjoying the cool air, country smells and cacophony of bird songs.

"It's time," said Mike. "Breakfast…oops…closer to lunch, actually… Let's call it 'lunfast'. What would you like for lunfast? I'm cooking. Want lunfast in bed or will you join me on the sun porch?"

"Sun porch. But I may stay in my jammies for lunfast."

Mike brewed a large pot of Costa Rican coffee, filled glasses with cold, fresh orange juice and set the table. As Marie lounged on the sun porch, Mike made a spinach salad with grapefruit slices, feta cheese, bright red tomatoes, topped with cranberries and toasted almonds.

"First course," said Mike as he put the colorful bowl in the middle of the table. "Dig in."

"This is wonderful, Mike. Thank you for pampering me today."

"Save space for the main course."

After the last spinach leaf was gone, Mike went back to the kitchen. Wonderful aromas filled the porch.

"That smells great. The neighbors may be over soon."

"And, for the lady… cheddar grits with shrimp and Andouille sausage," said Mike as he brought the steaming platter to the table.

"Wow. If I knew you could cook like this, we would have had role reversal many years ago," said Marie.

Mike and Marie lingered over the lunfast for almost two hours, talking about nothing, not Square One, and not Marie's big news. After cleaning the dishes, they walked around the lake. When they got to the playground they both laughed at the kids playing on the witch's hat, remembering Mike's big insight on their last trip.

"So much has happened since our last visit here," said Mike. "Watching the kids on the witch's hat made me see Square One differently. We sat here sketching witch's hats showing the need to create balance in so many aspects of the company. It was a really useful tool to communicate with the team. I think the company is spinning now. Maybe not as fast as it could, but definitely spinning. And, I really believe that in time, and maybe not that much time, the company will be spinning really fast."

"You've done an amazing job with the company, Mike. I couldn't be prouder!"

"I couldn't have done it without you at my side, Marie," said Mike as he enveloped her in his arms for a long hug.

"Mike, do you remember during our last visit I drew a witch's hat with another balance that we needed to have, Mike, Marie and Square One? How do you think that's going?"

"Oh, honey, you know that the balance between us is the most important one to me. I would never jeopardize it. When Don asked me to spend six months running the company, I had no idea what I was in for. It has been an incredible rollercoaster ride. There were times that I felt so overwhelmed. I appreciate that you were my only anchor. There were some amazing highs, when I felt like I could lead the company to a great future if you were at my side. My six months are almost over and I have to tell the Board if I want to continue or if I will start the search for the new President. What should I do, Marie?"

"I can't tell you what to do, Mike. I will support whatever you decide, but I want us both to commit to keeping our marriage a top priority, whatever that decision entails."

"Pinkey swear," said Mike as he and Marie linked little fingers.

"Before you decide what you want to do at Square One, Mike, there's one more witch's hat I want you to think about." Marie handed Mike her sketch.

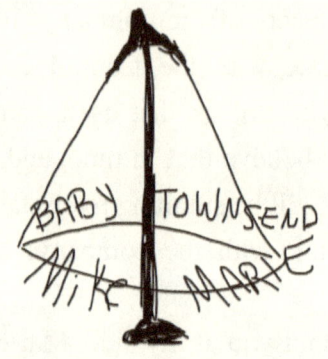

Mike stared at the picture in silence for several minutes. Then, he jumped from his seat and hugged Marie, smothering her with kisses. "Really? Really? When? How far along? How do you feel? Put your feet up. When did you know? Are you feeling OK? What can I do? What should we name her...or him? When will she ...or he...arrive? What color do you want the baby's room painted? I can start painting next weekend. Did you tell your mother yet?"

"Whoa, whoa, one question at a time," laughed Marie. Mike's obvious excitement erased Marie's doubts and concerns. He was already acting like a proud papa.

Mike and Marie spent the rest of the afternoon walking, talking and hugging.

"Darling, I know you were probably concerned that our baby would complicate my decision about Square One. Just the opposite. I now have complete clarity on what to do. I love you more than you realize!"

The Board Meeting

Mike had a glow on Monday morning that was impossible to hide. The weekend was just what he needed to reflect on his future and the role he wanted to play at Square One. He was nervous about the Board meeting scheduled for 7:00 pm, but also excited. He and Marie had expertly crafted his prepared speech and the accompanying letter.

The Board meeting opened with the usual camaraderie. The agenda followed the standard format with reports from the Chair, the Operations Report, the Marketing and Sales report, the Financial Statements and the Strategic Plan summary of progress against goals. Mike was scheduled to speak under new business near the end of the meeting. It was obvious that the Board members were watching Mike, trying to discern what direction he would go.

Finally, Anne turned to Mike. "Mike, it's been a challenging but rewarding six months. Before we hear your decision, I want to express on behalf of all of the Board members that we truly appreciate what you have accomplished at Square One. Don made the right decision when he selected you to fill the gap. Whatever your decision, we will support you."

Mike stood. He cleared his throat. He wished he had a pin to drop to prove the old saying.

"Thank you, Anne. And, thank you to all of the Board members. It has indeed been a challenging but rewarding six months. For me, it has been life changing. I admired Don. I respected him. And, yes, I loved him. Many of you know that he was the best man at my wedding. I miss him terribly. It was an honor to be named as his 'fill in' and to sit at his desk for the past six months. His letter to me challenged me to decide if I want to continue as President and to become an owner of the company or if I want to head a selection committee to find the new President. Today, I need to discuss with you my decision."

When Mike paused, the silence was palpable.

"This has not been an easy decision. First, I will admit to you that I was not sure that I was the right person for the job. I questioned whether or not I had the skill or brains to fill Don's shoes. I wasn't sure if the staff would develop trust in me or if you, the Board, would trust me in that role. I also had to consider my personal life. Marie and I are happy to announce that we are expecting our first child."

Applause and congratulations filled the room.

"I just found out about the baby on Saturday. Marie was afraid that it would make my decision harder. But, instead, it gave me great clarity. I know what I want to do. Now, I need to convince you, the Board, to support me in that decision."

Mike stopped talking and allowed the silence to fill the room. He smiled to himself as he thought about how he learned this technique from Sandy.

"The thing that I admired most about Don was who he was as a person, as a husband and as a member of the community. Although Anne stayed in the background, she was as much a part of the company as he was. This weekend I realized that what I loved most about Don is that he treated Square One as a true 'family business'. He ran the business to be successful, but for him the definition of successful was not only money. He felt successful when others were successful, his family and his extended family, all of the employees and their families. I realize that is the legacy that Don wanted completed. I want to be like

Don. I want the opportunity to try to fill his shoes. Now, as a brand new expectant father, I understand 'family' more than I ever did before. I am submitting to you a request to be considered for the position of President with the opportunity to become an owner of Square One."

Applause exploded.

Anne quickly stood. "Before you change your mind, I call for a vote of the Board."

"Aye, aye, aye, aye, aye, aye, aye.

"Congratulations, Mike. Welcome to the family!"

The Letter to Don

Mike walked out of the Board meeting in a daze. He couldn't help but touch his inside jacket pocket which held the letter he wrote to Don on the day of Don's funeral.

"Keep watching out for me, OK?"

My Dear Friend,

I miss you. I am both honored and touched by your confidence in me to finish your legacy. No, scared. I'm scared. I'm not sure I understand your legacy and I really don't want to let you down.

My promise to you is that I will do my best to fulfill your wishes. Keep an eye out and watch over me, OK?

Always,

Mike

Epilogue: Three Years Later

Marie, Mike and two and a half year old Donnie were walking around the lake in the Poconos.

"You realize that the last time we were here was when I told you about expecting Donnie? This place has such great meaning for us. My brother is a dear for sharing his vacation home and to encourage us to come here."

"Donnie is having the time of his life. Did you see his eyes light up when he saw the beach?"

During the past three years Mike, had led Square One through tough times, including an economic downturn and some significant changes in technology. But the team was solid and the company was on a good track. Most important, Mike kept his promises of keeping the company as a "family-oriented business".

As they continued their walk around the lake they came to the playground. Donnie made a beeline for the witch's hat.

"Chip off the old block," said Mike with a chuckle.

"Not for you yet, honey, you need to be a bit older for that one," said Marie as she directed the toddler toward the small slide.

"By the way, Mike, do witch's hats ever have four sides?"